475 TAX DEDUCTIONS

FOR ALL SMALL BUSINESSES, HOME BUSINESSES, AND SELF-EMPLOYED INDIVIDUALS

T0268066

Reviews

"This A-to-Z guide to hundreds of legitimate write-offs is like found money for business owners."

—Syndicated columnist Deborah L. Jacobs

"Amazingly, Kamoroff has made his ABC reference fun to read."

—InBusiness Magazine

"Accessible and user-friendly, this book is superbly presented and strongly recommended."

—Midwest Book Review

475 TAX DEDUCTIONS

FOR ALL SMALL BUSINESSES, HOME BUSINESSES, AND SELF-EMPLOYED INDIVIDUALS

PROFESSIONALS, CONTRACTORS, CONSULTANTS, STORES & SHOPS, GIG WORKERS, INTERNET BUSINESSES

Fourteenth Edition

Bernard B. Kamoroff, CPA

LYONS PRESS

Essex, Connecticut

An imprint of Globe Pequot, the trade division of
The Rowman & Littlefield Publishing Group, Inc.
4501 Forbes Blvd., Ste. 200
Lanham, MD 20706
www.rowman.com

Distributed by NATIONAL BOOK NETWORK

Copyright © 2024 Bernard B. Kamoroff, CPA

Quote from "Pretty Boy Floyd" by Woody Guthrie, courtesy Fall River Music
IRS Help Line cartoon, courtesy Bill Webster
IRS Files and Office photographs, courtesy Internal Revenue Service
Webster's World, courtesy Bill Webster
Sister Ruby cartoon, courtesy John Grimes
Don't You Dare Deduct Me cartoon, courtesy William Hamilton
Professional Writer cartoon, courtesy Mort Gerberg
Sacramento Tax Files photo by Dan Chan, courtesy Franchise Tax Board
King Kong cartoon, courtesy Kat Emerson
Most People Bring Their Accountant cartoon, courtesy Boardroom Reports
Gene Autry, courtesy of Michael Ochs
Man and cart cartoon by Bruce McCloskey

All rights reserved. No part of this book may be reproduced in any form or by any electronic
or mechanical means, including information storage and retrieval systems, without written
permission from the publisher, except by a reviewer who may quote passages in a review.

British Library Cataloguing in Publication Information available

Library of Congress Cataloging-in-Publication Data Available

ISBN 978-1-4930-7372-6 (paperback)
ISBN 978-1-4930-7852-3 (e-book)

∞™ The paper used in this publication meets the minimum requirements of American National
Standard for Information Sciences—Permanence of Paper for Printed Library Materials, ANSI/
NISO Z39.48-1992.

Please Read:

I have done my very best to give you useful and accurate information in this book, but I cannot guarantee that the information is correct or will be appropriate to your particular situation. Laws and regulations change frequently and are subject to differing interpretations. It is your responsibility to verify all information and all laws discussed in this book before relying on them. Nothing in this book can substitute for legal advice and cannot be considered as making it unnecessary to obtain such advice. Obtain specific information from the Internal Revenue Service or a competent person.

Thank You . . .

Larry Jacobs, Jan Zobel, Brad Walton, Stephen Fishman, Jim Angell, and Sharon Kamoroff.

Contents

"If you don't claim it, you don't get it. That's money down the drain for millions of Americans."

—Former IRS Commissioner Mark Everson

Preface:
A Treasure Hunt

Every business owner and every self-employed person is looking for ways to reduce expenses without cutting corners, without reducing quality or losing customers. But few businesses look to the one area almost guaranteed to save you money: your tax return.

Last year, according to a CPA study reported in *Business 2000,* America's small businesses overpaid their income taxes by more than $2 billion. The overpayments were made because the businesses failed to take tax deductions they were legally entitled to take. Many of these businesses are still unaware of their errors. They overpaid their taxes and don't even know it.

The IRS is not going to help these businesses. The IRS will never tell you about a tax deduction you didn't take. It's entirely up to you. As former IRS commissioner Mark Everson famously said, "If you don't claim it, you don't get it."

Whether you struggle with your own tax return, hire an accountant, or put your trust in a software app, the more you know about what's deductible, the more you'll save on your taxes. Your tax return lists only a handful of deductions, so it is up to you to make sure you find and claim every one. It really is a treasure hunt.

Every tax deduction you find in this book will reduce your taxes, honestly, legitimately, and with the full approval of the Internal Revenue Service.

It is very much like finding free money.

If the adjustments required by section 481 (a) and Regulation 1.481-1 are attributed to a change in method of accounting initiated by the taxpayer, the amount of such adjustments, to the extent such amount does not exceed the net amount which would have been required if the change had been made in the first taxable year, shall be taken into account by the taxpayer in computing taxable income in the manner provided in section 481 (b) (4) (B) and paragraph (b) of this section.

—Internal Revenue Code

*Well as through this world I've rambled
I've seen lots of funny men.
Some will rob you with a six-gun
And some with a fountain pen.*

—Woody Guthrie, "Pretty Boy Floyd"

1

Introduction to Tax Deductions

In America there are two tax systems, one for the informed and one for the uninformed. Both are legal.

—Judge Learned Hand

Relax

Relax. Tax law isn't easy, but this book is.

This book will not try to explain how to prepare a tax return. This book will not have you struggling with tax forms. This book will not drag you through the confusing, contradictory, confounding world of tax law.

This book *will* let you know about hundreds of tax deductions that are available to every small business, every home business, every self-employed individual, every independent contractor, and every gig-economy worker.

A CPA by the name of George Brown who was interviewed in a business magazine made a statement that has stuck with me for several years and that inspired this book: "You get a raise every time you can legitimately avoid paying a tax on something." Every tax deduction you find will save you money on your federal income taxes, on your state income taxes, on your self-employment taxes, on local income taxes, and on any other business taxes based on net profit.

If you really like the challenge of preparing your own tax return, I encourage you to do it. And if you don't want to struggle with tax forms, leave that miserable job to your tax accountant. Either way, you owe it to yourself to find every tax deduction you can.

Who Is This Book For?

This book is for anyone working for himself or herself. This includes sole proprietors, partners in partnerships, members of limited liability companies (LLCs), and people who own their own corporations.

This book is for shopkeepers, repair people, manufacturers, tradespeople, freelancers, professionals, independent contractors, outside contractors, subcontractors, general contractors, contract laborers, entrepreneurs, consultants, mail-order businesses, internet businesses, artists, craftspeople, direct marketers, network marketers, multilevel marketers, free agents, virtual assistants, sales reps, inventors, employers, moonlighters, home businesses, full-time, part-time, sideline, you name it. Unless you are on someone else's payroll as an employee, you are in business for yourself. You are entitled to all the business deductions in this book.

This book is for anyone who gets a 1099-NEC (non-employee compensation) form, which is an IRS "information return" that businesses give to individuals who are doing contract work but are not on the payroll as an employee.

This book is for on-demand workers in the gig economy: drivers, delivery people, house cleaners, service and repair people, and other contract workers getting assignments from smartphone-enabled platforms.

This book is for employers and for people who own their own corporation and are employees of their own business.

Investors: This book is for people who invest in their own businesses, but not for people who invest in other people's businesses. This book is for people who offer investment consulting or financial services or brokering related to investments.

This book is for traders in securities, people who regularly and repeatedly buy and sell securities (stocks, bonds) as a business. This book is *not* for people who occasionally invest in stocks or commodities or similar investments, who hold securities long term, who are not in the day-to-day world of buying and selling. These investors are not considered to be in business.

The difference between a trader who can deduct business expenses and an investor who cannot take the deductions might be a fine distinction in some cases. Investors who have a lot of money at stake, and a potentially large tax bill, are well advised to talk to an experienced accountant.

Rental income: Rental income may or may not be self-employment income. People who own hotels, motels, bed-and-breakfasts, and similar lodging businesses are self-employed. This income is reported as business income (on Schedule C for sole proprietors), *not* as rental income on Schedule E, Supplemental Income and Loss. People who manage property and rentals for others are self-employed.

People who own residential or commercial rental property and people who earn rental income from app-based services such as Airbnb are not usually considered to be self-employed. If, however, you are regularly putting in time on the rentals—collecting rent, maintenance, repairs, tenant services, leases, paperwork—and are treating the activity like a business, particularly keeping good records, the income can be considered as self-employment, and the deductions in this book will apply. The IRS has a guideline that people who devote at least 250 hours a year to rental activity are self-employed. People who spend fewer than 250 hours a year might also qualify depending on the level of involvement in the business. This is something I suggest you discuss with an experienced accountant.

People earning rental income who do not meet the qualifications for self-employment can still take a lot of the deductions in this book, as rental income on Schedule E.

Statutory employees and statutory non-employees: One strange category of self-employed individuals, actually two strange categories, are people the IRS calls statutory employees and statutory non-employees. In both of these cases, the "employees" file Schedule C tax forms and can take all of the tax deductions in this book.

Statutory employees include full-time life insurance salespeople; commission truck drivers who deliver laundry, food, or beverages other than milk; individuals working from their own homes who are hired by businesses to do work with materials provided by the businesses, typically seamstresses; and traveling salespeople working full-time selling to businesses (but not to consumers). Statutory employees are subject to regular employee Social Security and Medicare taxes and unemployment insurance, paid by whoever is hiring the employees, but otherwise are treated as outside contractors who can deduct the expenses listed in this book.

Statutory non-employees are certain commission salespeople: direct sellers, some delivery people selling consumer goods, licensed real estate agents, and some newspaper vendors. The IRS permits these salespeople to be classified as outside contractors if there is a written agreement stating that they are independent contractors and responsible for their own taxes.

These statutory and non-statutory employees who are not employees for tax purposes occupy an inexplicable corner of tax law, for reasons lost in the dustbin of long-ago legislation. *Delivering beverages other than milk?* "Curiouser and curiouser," as Alice said.

Performers: Independent and freelance actors, singers, musicians, and other performers are self-employed and entitled to all of the deductions in this book.

Some performers who are hired employees ("qualified performing artists" to use the IRS term), on a payroll with tax deductions and year-end W-2 forms, may be able to write off business-related expenses (the deductions in this book) even though the performers are not self-employed. Performers who meet the following four requirements can file IRS Form 2106, Employee Business Expenses, to claim the tax deductions:

1. Had total income for the year from all sources, not just performing, of $16,000 or less.
2. Worked as a performer for at least two employers during the tax year.
3. Was paid $200 or more from at least two employers ($200 or more per employer).
4. Incurred business expenses of more than 10% of the income earned from performing.

Authors and songwriters: If royalties from writing or songwriting are a regular and ongoing source of income, they are considered self-employment income. The income is reported on Schedule C of your tax return, like other sole proprietors. All the deductions in this book apply to you.

If royalty income is only occasional or a one-shot occurrence, the royalties can be classified as supplemental income on Schedule E, Supplemental Income and Loss. This is an important distinction because self-employment income is subject to self-employment tax, but supplemental income is not. Many of the deductions in this book are also deductible on Schedule E.

Songwriters who are also performers are generally considered to be self-employed, and the songwriting income is considered self-employment income. Most musician-songwriters combine both incomes under one business, one tax schedule.

Marijuana businesses: Businesses that grow, process or sell marijuana (or cannabis, the same thing) or products that contain or are made from marijuana, whether recreational or medical, are severely limited in what they can deduct on their federal tax returns, even in states that have legalized marijuana sales. The only expenses that are deductible are the cost of the marijuana and shipping or delivery charges to acquire it, and any state excise taxes levied on the marijuana. No other deductions, deductions allowed for all other types of businesses, can be deducted on your federal tax return.

Business Legal Structure

Different legal structures, how your business is legally set up, sometimes have different tax deduction rules. Most of the tax deductions in this book apply to all businesses, but some tax deductions apply to certain types of businesses and not to others. Any deductions that have different rules for different legal structures are labeled in bold. Here is a brief summary of the different legal structures.

Sole proprietorship: Most one-person businesses are sole proprietorships. If you did not incorporate or set up as a limited liability company (LLC), you are automatically a sole proprietor. All the deductions in this book except those specifically for businesses other than sole proprietorships apply to you.

Partnership: A business owned by two or more people (other than a married couple) that does not set up as a corporation or an LLC is automatically a partnership. A business owned by a legally married couple can be a partnership, following partnership tax rules, or can be what's known as a joint venture. See below.

There are three different legal structures that include the word *partnership*: general partnership, limited partnership, and limited liability partnership. They refer to different types of business arrangements with different tax laws. The typical small business partnership is a general partnership. The deductions in this book apply to all three types of business, but all references to partnerships in this book, unless otherwise specified, are for general partnerships.

Joint venture: A legally married couple who run a business can be a partnership or, at their option, a joint venture. In a joint venture, the two spouses run a single business but file two IRS Schedule Cs with their 1040 joint tax return, each spouse claiming half of the income and half of the expenses. For tax purposes the joint venture is two sole proprietorships, one for each spouse. The rules for joint ventures are the same as the rules for sole proprietorships.

Limited liability company: There is some confusion about taxation of LLCs because the IRS does not recognize the LLC as a separate business category and there is no federal LLC tax return. LLCs are treated as either sole proprietorships or partnerships, depending on how the LLCs are set up.

Multi-owner LLCs are taxed as partnerships, and the tax laws for partnerships apply.

Most one-person LLCs are taxed as sole proprietorships, and the tax laws for sole proprietorships apply. These one-person LLCs file a Schedule C tax form, Profit or Loss from Business, the same tax form used by sole proprietors.

However, some one-person LLCs choose to file taxes as a partnership, which is very uncommon. There is no tax benefit, and several drawbacks, to being a partnership instead of a sole proprietorship. But if your one-person LLC is structured as a partnership, the deductions in this book that apply to partnerships apply to you.

All references in the book to one-person LLCs assume that your business is taxed as a sole proprietorship.

Self-employed individuals: This is not really a legal structure. It is a term that encompasses sole proprietors, partners in partnerships, couples in joint ventures, and owners of one-person LLCs. All of these people are self-employed.

Corporation: People who structure their businesses as corporations are not what the IRS calls self-employed. They are employees of their businesses. Actually, they are owner-employees. Tax deductions for owner-employees of corporations are sometimes different than for other types of businesses. The rules for C corporations are often different than the rules for S corporations. The A-to-Z listings spell out each difference.

Also, I'm sure you know this, but a C corporation is different than a Schedule C tax form for self-employed people. Speedy readers might fly by a C, and miss or misread a deduction.

How to Use This Book to Your Best Advantage

This guide lists every business tax deduction I have encountered in my thirty years of tax practice, consulting, teaching, and running my own businesses. I let you know what the deductions are and whether they apply to you and your business.

Tax laws are precise, and I've tried to make this book as precise as possible, but without making it so confusing and complicated that it becomes unreadable—like most of the tax guides on the market. I've tried to accomplish this task with a three-step system:

Step One: For each tax deduction, the basic law is noted: Yes, it's deductible. No, it isn't deductible. Or maybe, it's deductible but with exceptions.

Step Two: Exceptions to the laws, limits or maximums, and any special situations for different types of businesses are highlighted and explained.

Step Three: If the law is complex, and for people who want more information, I refer you to one of the free IRS publications that have the fine-print details of the laws. However, for most deductions, this step is unnecessary. That's what this book is for.

Read carefully: The wording in tax law is important. The words have very specific meanings. Don't read more into the laws than what is explained here, don't read between the lines, and don't make assumptions, as you can easily wind up making assumptions that are inaccurate. Be particularly alert to terms such as "up to" and "as much as," which mean that the dollar amounts shown are maximums. These terms usually show up in complicated laws with many exceptions.

If any terminology is confusing or unclear—if you do not understand a word, a definition, or an explanation—it is important that you stop and take the time to understand its meaning before using the information. Misunderstanding tax law can lead to trouble. If you don't fully understand the concepts, get help from an accountant. Or do your own research—carefully.

Internet information: If you, like everybody else, are searching the internet for an answer, I want to warn you about tax information on the internet. Many websites have incorrect or out-of-date tax information. Even if you see the information multiple times on multiple sites, do not assume it is correct. Websites often lift information from other sites, sometimes word for word, without bothering to verify its accuracy. Even if you are reading information provided by tax professionals, check to see when the information was written. It might be several years old. If you can't find a date, don't trust it.

The most accurate, reliable tax information on the internet is on the IRS website, IRS.gov, although it can be a challenge to navigate the site. It's easiest to enter what you're looking for in a search engine and then look for links to the IRS.gov website. I wouldn't rely on any other site. Another caution: The website IRS.com is not the Internal Revenue Service. It is a commercial, privately owned site. The IRS web site ends in .gov.

Although the IRS website and publications are current and accurate, the same cannot always be said of tax information the IRS gives out over the phone or in person. The IRS people do, on occasion, give out totally incorrect information. Tax laws are vastly complicated, and even the experts make mistakes. Do not rely on verbal information unless you can verify it. Ask the IRS person for a reference in one of the agency's publications, and look it up.

Expense Categories

Every deduction listed in this book includes an expense category. The expense category is a guide to help you fill out your tax return, to figure out on what line of the tax return to post each deduction.

Schedule C, the business tax return for sole proprietors, lists only twenty-five categories of expenses, twenty-five line items. The partnership and corporate tax returns list a similar number of categories. And here we have 475 deductions to combine into twenty-five categories. Where do the 475 deductions go? What categories?

Some categories are obvious. Interest goes on the Interest line. Advertising goes on the Advertising line. Pencils go on the Office Expenses line. But where do you stick education expenses? Freight? Decorating expenses? Alarm systems? You can use the expense category designations in the book as a guide.

These expense categories are only a guide. They are not law, not rigid. It is not critical which deductions go on which lines on the tax form. The IRS is not going to be upset if an expense that belongs on one line winds up on another, especially low-cost items. Even I'm not sure whether some deductions should be labeled Office Expenses or Supplies or something else. If you have a deduction you don't know where to put on the tax return, just pick a reasonable category and put it there.

It is a good idea to make a worksheet showing which expenses you combined for the tax return and keep it with your copy of your return; no need to send it to the IRS. This will make things a lot easier should you ever face an audit, if you need to check your figures later, or if you are just looking back a year later trying to figure out how to fill out next year's tax return.

There is a line on the tax return called Other Expenses, used for deductions that don't fit into any other category. Many of the deductions in this book are shown as Other Expenses because there wasn't a more appropriate category on the tax return. Deductions you include in Other Expenses are listed individually, unlike other deductions that are combined on the tax return. The tax return provides a separate area for listing the Other Expenses deductions. List each expense separately, then show the total on the Other Expenses line on the return.

Just remember that the category you pick is not critical. What *is* critical is that you take every deduction you are entitled to, regardless of where you put it on the tax return.

Is Every Possible Tax Deduction Listed?

This list of 475 deductions is compiled from my studies of tax laws for thirty years (somebody's got to do it, right?), my background as a CPA, and my experience working directly with hundreds of different businesses of all types.

But still, I'd be a fool to say that I've listed every possible deduction there is. If you have a deduction not listed in this book, and if it meets the basic rules for all deductions (covered below), by all means take it. Or at least ask an accountant about it. And let me know about it too, will you? Maybe the next edition of this book will be called *476 Tax Deductions*.

Isn't This What You Pay Your Accountant For?

Here is the most important piece of information in this book: You have to find these deductions yourself. You are the only person who knows the ins and outs of your own business. You cannot rely 100% on your bookkeeper, your accountant, your attorney, your software, or the Internal Revenue Service.

Any experienced tax accountant will (or certainly should) know about every tax deduction listed in this book. But your accountant can't possibly take the time to ask you—and his or her 300 other tax clients—about every possible deduction you didn't know about or failed to include in your records and ledgers. Your accountant, especially during the three hectic months of "tax season," January 15 to April 15, is preparing a dozen or maybe two dozen tax returns a day. The accountant most likely wants to take your annual totals, totals you yourself have summarized from your records, or totals the accountant pulls off your accounting software, enter them into the computer, push Print, and collect his $300 fee. Next.

If you are expecting an accountant to actually sit down with you, discuss tax deductions in detail, study your business and your records, and find you savings, you should plan to do this well before tax preparation time. Even then, you really should not expect an accountant who does not work day to day in your business to be able to rattle off every possible tax deduction you may be entitled to.

Instead, spend a few hours with this book. Skim the A-to-Z list of deductions, and spot the ones that may apply to you. Then, if needed, ask your accountant about them. Your accountant will be of much greater help, and much greater value, if you first go through these 475 deductions before seeing the accountant. And by doing a little homework, you may significantly reduce the accounting fees.

Well-known tax attorney Julian Block said it best: "The informed client gets the best advice."

Will Your Deductions Trigger an Audit?

Are you afraid to take certain deductions because you fear they may trigger an audit? Welcome to the club. There are thousands of small businesses paying millions of dollars in taxes they don't owe, year after year, simply out of fear of being audited.

"Don't take the home business deduction, it'll guarantee an audit." What home business owner hasn't heard that? It is a myth. The home deduction does not invite an audit. And the same applies to most tax deductions.

But yes, there are a few tax deductions that are red flags, ones likely to bounce your return out of the computer, to put that nasty gleam in the eye of some IRS auditor, deductions that are likely to invite an audit, and yes, ones you may want to skip or at least be careful about when preparing your tax return.

Deductions that are likely to invite an audit are marked in bold **IRS Red Flag Audit Warning** in the A-to-Z list. They include large travel deductions; deductions for expenses not typically associated with your type of business; deductions for items of a personal or recreational nature; any large deductions out of line with the amount of income you are reporting. Although a home business deduction does not trigger an audit, a *large* home deduction combined with a small income does increase your chances of being audited.

What will increase your odds of being audited is not so much the deductions but other things on your tax return: Loss year after year, especially for people who also have earnings from a job. An occupation targeted by the IRS because of potential "abuse" (ease of cheating), particularly businesses that deal in cash such as laundromats, car washes, and hair salons.

Barter transactions. Any dealings in bitcoins or other cryptocurrency. Failing to report income that was reported to the IRS on a W-2 or a 1099 form. Claiming your dog as a dependent. Telling the IRS that the income tax is unconstitutional.

If you discover from reading this book that you have a tax deduction that may cause you trouble, it is up to you to decide how "aggressive" you want to be or how safe you want to be when claiming the tax deduction. I think this book will help you make those decisions. But I recommend that you talk to a tax accountant about your concerns. Any good accountant should be able to help you stay within your comfort zone.

I think that is the real key: your comfort. No amount of money is worth destroying your peace of mind. No tax saving is worth high blood pressure. But short of a sleepless night of IRS worries, if you are entitled to a tax deduction, take it. The laws were written to allow these deductions. The IRS says, Take the deductions, you don't owe the tax. If the government in its wisdom is allowing a deduction, you in your wisdom should take it.

When in Doubt, Deduct

Even after all the studying, talking to experts, and getting deep into the Internal Revenue Code, sometimes you still cannot be positive that a particular deduction is or isn't legitimate. The IRS says one thing, the Tax Court says the exact opposite, and your congressman, who dreamed up the law, is still on vacation. What do you do?

The answer depends on your own personality, how comfortable or uncomfortable you would be if you have to face an audit, and how much is at stake. If you are only going to save a few bucks but might get a Dear Taxpayer letter from the IRS, and maybe open up a Pandora's box you'd rather stay closed, it's not worth the risk.

But if you have nothing to hide and lots to save, I personally would go for it. Your chance of being audited, no matter what you deduct, is extraordinarily small. If you do get audited, the worst that can happen is the IRS will say "no dice" and demand the back taxes you'd owe anyway, plus interest. There is usually no penalty for making an honest mistake or a reasonable, though incorrect, interpretation of the law.

I want to make one thing clear throughout this book. If any deduction is questionable, if there is any doubt, any disagreement, any IRS opposition, I spell that out in the description of the deduction. You will not be caught by surprise, you will not have to wonder whether a certain deduction can lead to possible trouble.

Tax Loopholes and Tax Secrets

Tax laws are often carelessly written. Every time a new tax law comes out, clever accountants and eagle-eyed lawyers find holes in the laws, find unintended deductions, and find ways around the laws neither Congress nor the IRS intended: tax "loopholes."

Some of these tax loopholes are legitimate, some are not, and some are what we call "gray" or questionable areas of tax law. In this book, every tax loophole that applies to business is listed and explained, so you will know which ones are legitimate deductions, which ones are questionable, and which ones are not deductible.

Do you want to know about tax secrets? There are none. There are no secrets in tax law. There are, however, legitimate tax deductions that few people know about, sort of a secret I guess. Every "secret" deduction that applies to business is in this book.

What isn't in this book are "tax avoidance" schemes, "abusive" tax shelters, tax scams, or dubious deductions that will get you audited. We are not out to deceive the Internal Revenue Service or anyone else. Some of the deductions listed in this book may be "tax loopholes" or "tax secrets," but they are genuine, acceptable, IRS-approved tax deductions. And each and every one is money in your pocket that stays in your pocket.

Federal versus State Laws

The laws explained in this book are federal tax laws for preparing your federal tax return. Many states have the exact same laws as the IRS, and most business deductions allowed on your federal return are allowed on your state return. But that is not guaranteed. You should study the instructions that come with your state tax forms or state tax publications or ask an accountant. You might find additional state deductions the IRS does not allow, and save even more money on your state taxes.

Keeping Records

Many legitimate tax deductions are lost because people don't know about them. That's the reason for this book. But many tax deductions are lost simply because people failed to record them. People who do not keep good records cheat themselves out of deductions because they didn't write them down. Recordkeeping is, in fact, the very heart of taking advantage of tax deductions.

If you don't have a good set of financial records, STOP. If you do not have a good system for recording every business expense, STOP. Get a set of paper ledgers, or set up a spreadsheet, or get accounting software or a smartphone app, and learn how to use it. If you are confused or don't understand recordkeeping, hire an accountant or a bookkeeper to help you set up your records and teach you the basics. Or read my book *Small Time Operator: How to Start Your Own Business, Keep Your Books, Pay Your Taxes, and Stay Out of Trouble.* There is an entire section devoted to setting up and keeping good financial records.

Get receipts for everything you possibly can, set up a good filing system for the receipts, and keep the receipts at least three years. Three years from the date you file your tax return is the IRS statute of limitations for most audits. Receipts are your best proof if the IRS ever challenges a deduction. If you don't have receipts, make notes about expenses or keep a business diary. Print copies of your bank statement and debit and credit card charges. Record mileage. And don't forget all those tiny out-of-pocket expenses. Even small purchases can add up to a significant tax deduction.

The IRS says that business records can be kept on paper or stored on your computer or disk or flash drive, or on the internet or a provider's server or cloud, as long as the information can be retrieved if the IRS requests it.

When Can You Take a Deduction?

Most deductions are taken the year you incur the expense. But there are exceptions to this rule. Some prepaid expenses are deducted the year they apply to, regardless of when they are paid. Some expenses are depreciated or amortized, which means they are written off over several years. In the A-to-Z list of deductions, any expense that cannot be deducted currently is explained.

Before starting a business: Expenses incurred before a business is actually open and earning income come under different deduction laws than expenses after the business is operating. These expenses are known as "Startup" expenses, though they really are pre-Startup expenses. Startup expenses, and when they can be deducted, are explained in the A-to-Z list.

Cash Method versus Accrual Accounting

Part of understanding when an expense can be deducted requires you to know about the two methods of accounting allowed by the IRS: the cash method and the accrual method. Almost all small businesses choose the cash method because it is easy to understand and requires much simpler recordkeeping.

Under the cash method, also called cash basis, expenses are recorded when paid (though with some exceptions). Purchases and commitments you've made but haven't yet paid for are not recorded in your expense records and are not deducted on your tax return until paid.

The cash method does not mean that all your transactions are in cash. Don't let the word *cash* confuse you. The cash method has nothing to do with how you pay your bills, only when you can deduct payments. Any business with annual sales of $27 million or less can use either the cash method or accrual method, your choice.

Under the accrual method, all expenses are recorded whether paid or not. An expense you incur this year but do not pay until next year is recorded as this year's expense and taken as a tax deduction this year, not next year when the bill is paid. It is the exact opposite of the cash method, much more complicated, and for most small businesses unnecessary.

Every IRS law is guaranteed to have exceptions, and the cash method is, well, no exception. Certain expenses cannot be deducted when paid, even for cash-method businesses. When you look up an expense item in the A-to-Z list, the entry will tell you if the expense cannot be deducted currently and when it can be deducted.

Structuring Transactions to Your Best Tax Advantage

Some business expenses are deductible, and some aren't. Often simply the way you structure a deal, the way you word a contract, or how you describe an expense can mean the difference between something that is deductible and something that isn't.

Throughout the book, I try to warn you about expenditures that can be interpreted or structured in different ways so that you'll be able to make the tax laws work for you. And it is perfectly legal. Large corporations hire $400-per-hour tax attorneys to do nothing but find ways around the taxes they don't want to pay. You get to buy this book. But don't be afraid to quiz your tax accountant about any expense that may want a little "reworking."

Regardless of the wording or the deductibility of an expense, business transactions should not solely be tax motivated. How many times have you heard about some business that is losing money or making a worthless purchase or spending frivolously but, hey, it's a tax write-off? After thirty years of dealing with tax laws, I still don't find logic in this strategy. The concept of incurring an expense solely as a tax write-off is, when you get right down to it, ridiculous. The expense will always be greater than the write-off the expense brings. That must be obvious. (A tax write-off and a tax deduction are the same thing.) Make sure an expense has a real purpose independent of tax consequences. Then figure out how to structure the deal to your best tax advantage. Don't let the taxes wag the dog.

Timing Transactions to Your Best Tax Advantage: Year-End Strategies

As the end of the year approaches, you can plan your business transactions to increase or decrease your profit, and therefore increase or decrease the taxes you will pay. Within limits, you can postpone or accelerate purchases and other business expenses.

For example, if you are thinking of buying a new computer, you can buy it in December for a deduction this year, or buy it in January for a deduction next year. You can do the same with most office equipment, machinery, inventory, supplies, maintenance, and repairs.

If you are on the cash method of accounting, you can prepay some of next year's expenses and get a deduction this year instead of next year. Or you can postpone paying some of this year's bills until next year if you would rather get the deduction next year.

If the current year is a low-income year, and if you already have enough deductions to bring your taxes down and keep your tax bracket at the minimum, you would probably benefit from postponing expenses to next year. If, on the other hand, this is a high-income year and you could use more deductions to reduce your tax burden, accelerating expenses, spending the money this year instead of next year, may be the best tax strategy.

You have right up to December 31 to make a purchase or expenditure that you can deduct for the current year. Once it's New Year's Day, it's too late.

Year-end payments: Checks that are mailed or delivered by December 31 can be deducted the year written, even if cashed in the new year. Automatic payments and any other bills paid electronically are deducted the year the payment is processed. Expenses on debit cards are deducted the year incurred.

Expenses charged to credit cards (MasterCard, VISA, Discover, American Express) are deducted the year the expense is incurred, even if paid next year. But expenses on charge cards issued by individual stores and gasoline companies cannot be deducted until paid (except for businesses on the accrual method of accounting). This curious rule is typical of a lot of IRS laws: unnecessarily complicated regulations that business owners hate and tax accountants love.

Paying Business Expenses: You or Your Business?

Who actually pays for a business expense—you the owner, or the business itself—can affect the deductibility of the expense. Much depends on how the business is structured.

If your business is a sole proprietorship, a one-person LLC, or a joint venture (married couple in business together), it does not matter whether you or your business pays the bills. If an expense is business related, your business gets the deduction. Cash you pay out of your pocket for a business expense is deductible. You can make business purchases on a personal credit card or debit card and get a business deduction. The card does not have to be in the business name. You can write a check on your personal bank account for business-related purchases and deduct them as business expenses. Your business vehicle does not have to be registered in the business name. A building or other business location that you own or rent does not have to be in the business name. You still get the deduction.

If your business is a partnership, corporation, or multi-owner LLC, the laws are very different. Business deductions are sometimes disallowed when claimed by the owners of the business instead of by the company itself. Try not to pay business expenses out of your personal funds. If you do pay any business expenses out of your own pocket or from your personal credit or debit card, have the business reimburse you so that the business itself can claim the deductions. But be careful: Business reimbursements have their own set of IRS rules, requiring a written reimbursement policy, called an "accountable plan." See Reimbursements in the A-to-Z list.

Multiple Businesses

If you have more than one business, the IRS requires that you keep separate records and file separate tax forms for each business. You could instead choose to have only one business with different "departments" or "divisions." With one business, you need to keep only one set of records and file one tax return.

If you do set up separate businesses, shared expenses that apply to both businesses such as office space, computer, telephone, or employees working for both businesses should be prorated between the businesses, 50–50 or any other split that reasonably approximates usage.

Home-Based Businesses

As far as the IRS is concerned, a home-based business is no different than any other business. Home business owners file business tax returns, report the earnings as business income, and deduct business expenses. The expenses that home-based businesses can deduct are exactly the same as the expenses every other business can deduct, with one important exception: the home itself.

If you use part of your home for business—your office, workshop, store, warehouse, or whatever you are using your home for—the cost of the space (the rent or, if you own your home, the depreciation) and some of the expenses directly related to the space such as utilities and maintenance can be deducted only if the space meets special IRS requirements. The requirements are explained under Home Expenses in the A-to-Z listing.

The requirements are not difficult to understand and are very easy to meet for most home-based businesses. Still, lots of home businesses do not take the deduction because of a widespread belief that deducting your home office or workspace is likely to lead to an audit. Which is not true. The IRS does not audit home businesses any more than other small businesses, at least not home businesses that report a profit.

The IRS is more likely to audit a home business if the business has a loss, especially if the loss is offsetting other income and reducing income taxes. Auditors are suspicious, often correctly, that the money-losing home business is not really a business at all but a hobby or some pursuit or fun project that you're trying to write off on your tax return. The IRS is also more likely to audit a home business, or any business for that matter, that takes large deductions for expenses like travel and other "fun" types of expenses, the red flag deductions in the A-to-Z listings.

So the message here, and throughout the book, is: Don't worry about the IRS. Deduct everything you are entitled to.

I mention this in the Home Expenses listing, but it bears repeating: If you do not qualify for the home expense deduction, it does not prohibit you from operating your business out of your home or deducting business expenses. It only means that one possibly large expense, the cost of the home itself and the expenses related to the home, such as utilities, are not deductible on your federal income taxes. You can still deduct all legitimate business expenses other than those directly related to the business space.

There actually is one other tax deduction, in addition to the home expense deduction, that is limited for home businesses. The cost of a landline telephone into the home cannot, in some cases, be deducted. It's a mean-spirited little law that's getting slowly obsolete as more and more businesses are switching to smartphones and internet-connected phones, which do not come under this landline law. See Telephones in the A-to-Z listing.

Other business use of the home: The home expenses deduction applies not just to businesses that are home based but also to any business where the owner of the business uses his or her home for business purposes. Many mobile businesses, businesses that travel to customers, quality for the home expenses deduction. Contractors, salespeople, entertainers, freelancers, consultants, and others who earn income outside the home may be eligible for the home expenses deduction. Even businesses that have separate business locations outside the home may be eligible for the deduction. The IRS rules for deducting home expenses are explained under Home Expenses in the A-to-Z list.

Gig Workers

The gig economy—the on-demand economy, the sharing economy—has become successful, at times extraordinarily successful, because the gig businesses ("platforms") found a loophole in the law to eliminate the number-one biggest expense most businesses face: employees, and all the costs, paperwork, and employment laws associated with hiring employees.

The gig workers—on-demand workers, contract workers (Uber calls them partners, though the workers are not partners in any legal sense)—are what the IRS calls independent contractors or contract labor. The workers are not legally employees, which lets the gig businesses operate without paying any of the costs required of regular employers: payroll taxes, workers' compensation insurance, unemployment taxes, health insurance coverage. No vacation pay, no holiday pay, no overtime pay, no sick leave. On-demand companies do not have to comply with minimum wage laws, employment safety laws, discrimination laws, or termination laws. On-demand companies refer to themselves as disruptors. They've disrupted a legal system that was put in place to protect employees and to protect consumers.

Whether you love the disrupters or hate them or just don't care, the bottom line is that if you are an on-demand worker, you are in business for yourself. You are, no matter what you or anyone else calls you, self-employed. Every tax deduction in this book applies to you.

Legally, gig workers are sole proprietors. You file a sole proprietorship tax form, Schedule C, Profit or Loss from Business, that attaches to your 1040 income tax return. You report your income from your gig work, combined with the income from any other related self-employment, on Schedule C. You deduct your expenses, and pay income tax on the profit.

1099 workers: Gig workers are sometimes called 1099 workers, which refers to IRS form 1099-NEC, Non-employee Compensation. The gig companies are required to prepare 1099-NEC forms for every worker who received $600 or more in a calendar year.

For the worker, however, it does not matter whether you get a 1099 form or not. It does not matter whether you earned $600 or not. If you are getting paid by a gig economy platform, you are an independent contractor. You are self-employed. You file a Schedule C tax form. You do not need a 1099 form; you do not file the 1099 form with your tax return. If a gig business was required to issue a 1099 form to you but didn't, that is not an issue or a problem for you. You pay taxes on what you earned, 1099 form or not. And as I mentioned above, and mention again, every deduction in this book applies to you.

Home expenses deduction: One important tax deduction that gig workers should know about is the home expenses deduction. Self-employed individuals can get a tax deduction for having an office in their home, which can reduce your taxes significantly.

You don't have to actually be doing your work in your home to get the deduction. You can be working in a client's home, or driving your car or whatever else the on-demand platforms contract you to do, and still get the home expenses deduction. You do have to comply with certain IRS requirements, but they are easy to meet. Read the Home Expenses entry in the

A-to-Z listing, and set up your office and your business scheduling to meet the IRS requirements.

Occasional work: Some gig workers are working only occasionally, not regularly earning money. These workers are *not* self-employed according to the IRS. Self-employed individuals are people who work, to quote the IRS, "with a reasonable degree of regularity." Occasional on-demand income does not meet this requirement. The income is taxable, but you cannot take any business deductions.

This is a real problem for workers with occasional income, as the IRS does not define what they call "a reasonable degree of regularity." I definitely suggest that you talk to an experienced (and sympathetic) tax accountant. This law does not apply to self-employed people who earn money from several different sources, of which on-demand income is only a part. You report all your income on one Schedule C tax form, and you can claim all your deductible expenses.

Hobby Income and Losses

Hobbies are not businesses. Income from a hobby is not self-employment income. Any income earned from a hobby is taxable, but the expenses are not deductible. To take full advantage of the tax laws, you want to be sure your business is in fact a real business and not just a hobby earning a few bucks. More important, if your business is showing a loss, you don't want the IRS to rule that the business isn't a business, no loss allowed. A business that is a real business and not a hobby can show a loss and be able to use that loss to offset other income in figuring your taxes.

When is an endeavor a hobby, and when is it a business? The IRS has specific rules defining what is and isn't business income. In chapter 3, "The Four Basic Rules for All Expenses," Rule 1 spells out the IRS requirements.

The IRS also has what they call the Hobby Rule, or the Three-Year/Five-Year Rule. If you do not show a profit for at least three out of five consecutive years, the IRS can declare your business to be a hobby and disallow business deductions and any losses. This is not a firm rule, however. A business can deduct losses for several years in a row without being challenged by the IRS. In the event of an audit, the IRS will allow the ongoing losses if they are convinced that you are operating a real business and trying, though unsuccessfully, to make a profit.

The key issue is *intent*. What are you really doing? Trying to earn some money or just having fun? It will help if your business looks like a business—licenses, financial records, bank account, internet presence— and if you're devoting time to it in a businesslike manner.

Year-to-Year Changes

Most tax deductions stay the same year after year. It is extraordinarily unusual for an expense to be deductible one year and not deductible the next. However, the amounts that are deductible, the maximums, the percentages, often change every year or every two or three years. You should verify these amounts with a current IRS publication or the IRS.gov website.

What does occasionally change is a nondeductible expense that is challenged in Tax Court, and the court rules against the IRS, allowing the deduction. A few deductions listed in the A-to-Z list are the result of Tax Court rulings, rulings the IRS often refuses to acknowledge. If there is an issue with any deduction—the IRS says one thing, the courts say another—that is clearly spelled out in the listing.

"I Wish I Had This Book Last Year": Amending Prior Years' Tax Returns

Did you miss some deductions on last year's tax return that you were entitled to? Well, as some newspaperman said many years ago, Yes, Virginia, there is a Santa Claus.

You can go back and amend prior tax returns and claim a refund of prior years' taxes. Amended tax returns must be filed within three years from the date you filed your original return or within two years from the time you paid your tax, whichever is later. A return filed early is considered filed on the due date. So for 2024 tax returns filed and paid on time (April 15, 2025), you have until April 15, 2028, amend the return.

Tax returns are amended on form 1040-X for sole proprietorships and one-person LLCs, 1120-X for regular corporations, 1120-S (marked "Amended") for S corporations, and 1065 (marked "Amended") for partnerships and multi-owner LLCs. Refunds are fairly prompt. Amended returns are not more likely to be audited than original returns. If your federal return was in error, your state return was probably also in error. States have similar procedures for amending returns.

One Last Caution

Verify what you read in this book with a current IRS publication or with a competent accountant. Tax laws change every year. Congress is constantly screwing around with the tax laws. As soon as they pass another confusing law (and promptly go on vacation), the IRS starts issuing interpretations of the law. And then some clever tax attorney finds a loophole, and the Tax Court gets to put in its two cents. Pretty soon, the law means something different than it did a few months ago.

The word once printed cannot be altered. Tax law, however, changes constantly. As the wise old carpenter says, Measure twice, cut once.

2
Terminology

There are many different terms for the same thing. Ten different businesses in ten different states may have ten different terms for a given business expense. To make this book as easy as possible to use, I have tried to list every term I know for every business deduction.

For example, you can look up Goodwill and find that it is also known as Blue Sky. You can look up Blue Sky and find it is also known as Goodwill. Business Assets are also listed as Fixed Assets and Depreciable Assets. This system results in some repetition and duplication of definitions and explanations, but I think it makes the book faster and easier for people to use, and it eliminates the need to spend time poring over an index.

Here are a few important definitions you should know before getting any deeper into this book.

Self-Employed Individuals and Independent Contractors

Throughout this book you will see the term *self-employed individuals*. Self-employed individuals are in business for themselves. They are sole proprietors, partners in partnerships, and member/owners of limited liability companies (LLCs). Freelancers, consultants, building contractors, subcontractors, contract laborers, gig workers, free agents, and other people in an independent trade or profession are self-employed individuals.

The IRS often refers to self-employed people as independent contractors. The term *independent contractor* does not refer to being a building contractor. Independent means you are not someone's employee. Contractor means you are doing contract labor, another IRS term for self-employment. Independent contractors are also known as outside contractors. They mean the same thing.

There is an important distinction between self-employed individuals and people who set up their businesses as corporations. People who own corporations, both regular C corporations and S corporations, are employees of their businesses. Although they are obviously self-employed, the IRS does not refer to them as self-employed individuals, and neither does this book. Owners of their own corporations are referred to as employees or, if a distinction is important, as owner-employees.

Home Business/Home-Based Business

These two terms are used interchangeably in the book, but there is an important distinction. Many self-employed people work outside the home—contractors, tradespeople, consultants, salespeople—but have an office or shop or storage in their home. These people are eligible for the same tax home-office deductions as people operating businesses in their homes. All references to home business and home-based business apply to both.

Employer/Employee

As you go through this book, be careful reading the last letter of these two words. The employer hires the employee. The employee works for the employer. The employer-employee relationship is a formal, legal relationship, with specific tax consequences. Tax deductions for employers are very different than for employees.

Independent contractors, contract laborers, and other self-employed individuals are not employees. If you hire these people, you are not their employer. If you are an independent contractor, the person or company hiring you is not your employer.

If you are the owner of your own corporation, you *are* an employee of the business. In fact, you are both employer and employee, as I explained above under Self-Employed Individuals and Independent Contractors.

This book is careful to distinguish between employers, employees, and self-employed individuals. You are cautioned to be equally careful.

Tax Deduction or Tax Write-Off

These two terms mean the same thing. A tax deduction/tax write-off is a business expense that is subtracted from your total business income, your total sales, in order to arrive at your taxable income, your net profit.

A tax deduction—also called an allowable business expense, with an emphasis on "allowable"—is what you can deduct, not necessarily what you spend. While most expenses are deductible the year paid, some expenses are deducted over several years even though the payment was made all in one year. Some expenses are only partially deductible. You may have a $100 expenditure but only a $50 tax deduction because only half the expense is allowed by tax law. There are also business expenses, totally legitimate business expenses, that are not deductible at all.

This book explains which expenses are fully deductible the year paid, which expenses are deductible over several years, which expenses are only partly deductible, and which expenses are not deductible at all. I have listed every possible business expense whether it is deductible or not.

Schedule C

Schedule C, Profit or Loss from Business, is the IRS tax form that sole proprietors use to report their business income and expenses. It attaches to the taxpayer's 1040 tax return. Not to be confused with C corporation.

C Corporations and S Corporations

The IRS recognizes two types of corporations: C corporations, which sometimes are just called corporations without the C; and S corporations, which are also known as Sub S or Subchapter S corporations, Subchapter S being a section of the Internal Revenue Code that defines the S corporation.

The tax deduction laws for the two types of corporations are sometimes different, particularly for money paid to the owners of the corporations, and for health insurance deductions for the owners and their families.

Throughout the book, any difference in tax laws for C versus S corporations is spelled out.

B corporation: There is a type of corporation known as a B corporation, also called a benefit corporation, a designation that has no legal status. *B corporation* is a term coined by a private nongovernment organization to promote businesses that meet certain environmental or social objectives. All B corporations are either C corporations or S corporations. There are no B corporation laws.

Personal versus Business

A personal expense is a nonbusiness expense. It is not deductible on a business tax return. Expenditures that are partly personal and partly business can be prorated. The business portion is deductible.

The term *personal* also has a second, completely different meaning in tax law. Personal property is any tangible property other than real estate. Personal property includes machinery, equipment, furniture, and other assets a business owns. This personal property is actually business property, a business expense.

The difference between personal expense (not a business expense, and not deductible) and personal property (deductible business assets) is obviously very important, but you don't have to keep remembering it. Throughout the book, I point out the differences as they come up.

Capitalized Expenses

Capitalize is a tax term that means the cost of an asset is deducted over a period of years instead of being deducted the year incurred. Most buildings have to be capitalized. Most business assets other than buildings (machinery, equipment, furniture, vehicles) can be capitalized or, at your option, can be deducted the year of purchase.

Assets that are capitalized are written off using a procedure called depreciation or amortization, two terms that mean the same thing, except that depreciation is used for tangible assets (physical assets), and amortization is used for intangible assets such as patents, copyrights, and trademarks.

"Significant" Costs

IRS rules often distinguish between significant costs and insignificant costs, between major expenses and minor expenses. Insignificant or minor expenses often can be deducted currently. The IRS calls it, in their delightful way of communicating, a "de minimis safe harbor election." Significant or major expenses may have to be depreciated over several years.

The IRS generally considers anything costing under $2,500 to be insignificant, but that amount is not fixed in law except for a few specific deductions. Most businesses I know consider $2,500 to be quite significant, but if the IRS is okay with a deduction, so am I.

If you have employees, one "significant" issue to be careful about is the value of gifts or special benefits for your employees. The IRS is always on the lookout for "disguised compensation": paying employees in some form other than money in an attempt to avoid payroll taxes. This is an area of law that has much more rigid rules, and much more IRS scrutiny, than how you write off an asset. The $2,500 guideline does *not* apply here. But don't worry. Throughout the book, I guide you under the radar: no questionable deductions that might attract an auditor.

Customers, Clients, Etc.

A local drinking establishment in the town where I live has a sign behind the bar: "The customer is always right. But the bartender decides who is still a customer."

Different types of businesses have different terms for the people who buy their goods or services. Regardless of the terminology you prefer—customer, client, patron, guest, passenger, patient, student, subscriber—for tax law, all the terms are interchangeable.

Throughout the book, I use the word *customer*, sometimes *client* or other term for variety, to refer to whoever is buying whatever you're selling. I mean no disrespect to doctors or teachers or others who have specific terms to describe the people they serve. I'm just trying to keep the explanations, and the sentences, short.

IRS Audits

Throughout the book, I warn you about any deductions that might trigger IRS audits, and potential audit situations you might want to discuss with an accountant. Look for the bold **IRS Red Flag Audit Warnings**.

What's your chance of being audited? Every year the IRS selects a small percentage—actually a very small percentage, under 1%—of business tax returns to examine, looking to prove that the returns are accurate, that income is correctly stated, and that deductions are legitimate. IRS agents accomplish this task by talking to you or your accountant, by looking at your business records, and by examining your bank records and business receipts.

Some audits are extensive, examining your entire business operation for the year. Most audits, however, are narrowly focused, questioning only one or a few deductions. Some audits are done in person, but most audits are conducted through the mail or over the phone. At the conclusion of the audit, the IRS will report their findings and let you know if your tax bill increased, decreased, or remained unchanged.

Once you see the results of the audit, you can decide to accept or appeal the outcome. If your taxes went up a little, I suggest just paying the extra amount even if you think the IRS is not correct. It's never worth the time and hassle to argue with the IRS over a few dollars. If, however, the tax bill has jumped significantly, and if you think the IRS made a mistake, you can appeal directly, or you might do much better to hire an experienced tax accountant to give you some advice.

Quite often the IRS will find an error on a tax return when processing the return, typically an adding mistake or a tax calculation mistake. The IRS will automatically correct your return and notify you of your error and the increase or decrease in taxes. This kind of correction is not an audit. It does not increase or decrease your chances of being audited.

By the way, the term *audit* is no longer officially used by the IRS. According to the latest IRS press release, the IRS no longer audits tax returns. They, ah, conduct examinations. The examinations, however, are identical to what the IRS used to call audits. Why the euphemism, I do not know. Fish is fish. An audit is an audit. And one of the goals of this book is to help you avoid an audit. Or an examination.

Tax Credits versus Tax Deductions

Tax credits are different from tax deductions, and you should know the difference. A tax deduction reduces your net profit from your business. A tax credit does not reduce your business profit, but it does reduce your income taxes. An item is either a tax deduction or a tax credit, not both. The difference is quite important.

You compute your business net profit by taking your total income and subtracting your tax deductions. You figure your tax based on this net profit. After you compute your taxes, you then use tax credits to reduce those taxes.

A tax credit is much more valuable than a tax deduction. A tax deduction of $1,000 might save you $300 or $400 in taxes, depending on your tax bracket. But a tax credit of $1,000 will save you a full $1,000 in taxes. The tax credit is a little gold mine, it is.

Why does Congress offer both tax deductions and tax credits? To confuse the issues, of course. To make life more complicated for people trying to figure their taxes. To make accountants and tax lawyers rich. And because no one in Congress does his own tax return and has no idea how confusing the tax laws are. That's why.

That's not why. Most tax deductions are actual business expenses, the actual costs of running a business. Tax deductions tend to stay the same year after year. Many tax credits have nothing to do with the actual expense of running a business. They are instead tax breaks to encourage you to do socially responsible things like hire people to get them off welfare, or purchase equipment or vehicles that will make for cleaner air and water. Some tax credits are meant to stimulate the economy. And some, believe it or not, just give you a much needed tax break, period.

So send a letter of thanks to your congressman or congresswoman for the health insurance tax credit, small employer tax credit, tuition tax credit, research and development tax credit, oil drilling tax credit (that's right), and whatever else they've given us, or their corporate buddies, for Christmas this year.

Unlike tax deductions, tax credits tend to come and go, available one year and not the next. Congress has discovered that it is much easier to end a tax credit than it is to drop a long-standing tax deduction.

In this book, tax credits are specifically labeled as such. If an item in this book does not say it is a tax credit, it is a tax deduction. If it doesn't say whether it is a tax deduction or a tax credit, it is a tax deduction. Read carefully.

3

The Four Basic Rules
for All Expenses

Some business tax deductions are specifically spelled out in the IRS tax code: yes, you can deduct this; no, you cannot deduct that. But the great majority of business deductions, most of the tax deductions listed in this book, are not mentioned anywhere in the IRS code books. The law does not say, for example, that you can or cannot deduct pens for the office, light bulbs for the warehouse, or bank service charges.

What the IRS does say, and say adamantly, is that all business expenses, whether spelled out in the IRS code books or not, must meet four basic rules in order to be deductible:

1. The expenses must be incurred in connection with your trade, business, or profession.
2. The expenses must be ordinary.
3. The expenses must be necessary.
4. The expenses must not be lavish or extravagant under the circumstances.

Any expense that does not meet all four of these requirements cannot be deducted on your business tax return.

The four basic rules, however, are not always as basic as they sound (of course). It is important to understand these rules and, most important, to understand the definitions of the words as they are used in tax law. If you will take five minutes to read these definitions, you will have a much greater understanding of tax law and what you can legitimately deduct on your tax return.

Rule 1: Business Related

The expenses must be incurred in connection with your trade, business, or profession. The words *trade, business,* and *profession* are used interchangeably. All three refer to an activity, to quote the IRS, "carried on with a reasonable degree of regularity" and "sincere attempt to make a profit." It includes business owners and all self-employed individuals, freelancers, independent contractors, and independent professionals. It includes home businesses and people earning a living as on-demand workers.

"Reasonable degree of regularity" rules out occasional activities that bring in a little income. Such occasional activities are not considered a trade or business by the IRS. Part-time, seasonal, and pop-up businesses qualify if they are an ongoing activity.

"Sincere attempt to make a profit" rules out hobbies and other ventures done purely or mostly for the fun of it. There needs to be a real profit motive or the IRS says it is not a trade or business.

The expression "in connection with your trade or business" also means that you have already started a business. You must actually be in business before you are allowed to write off business expenses. You are not allowed a deduction for business expenses incurred in connection with a business you are thinking of starting, planning to start someday, or researching in anticipation of starting, until you have actually started the business, opened your doors, made your first sale. At that point, some of the pre-opening expenses can be deducted. See Startup Costs and, if you are starting a corporation, Organizational Costs in the A-to-Z list.

Expenditures that are partly personal (nonbusiness) and partly business can be prorated. The business portion is deductible.

Rule 2: Ordinary Expenses

The expenses must be ordinary. An ordinary expense is one that is common or accepted in your type of business. Ordinary expenses do not have to be recurring or habitual.

Rule 3: Necessary Expenses

The expenses must be necessary. A necessary expense, according to the IRS, is one "that is appropriate and helpful in developing and maintaining your trade or business."

The word *necessary* in this context does not have the same definition we usually associate with necessary, as in essential, indispensable, must be done. It is not necessary that you buy nice furniture. It is not necessary that you air-condition your office. These are not mandatory requirements of your business, but they pass the necessary test. An expense only has to be "appropriate and helpful" to meet the necessary test.

An important part of the necessary test is whether there is an "economic justification" for an expense, a good business reason to claim the deduction. This sometimes comes into play when an owner of a business is deducting payments that only benefit the owner or the owner's family. Owner-employees of corporations who take advantage of employee fringe benefits are sometimes denied the deductions, the IRS claiming there is no economic justification for the payments. This is definitely a foggy area of tax law, worth discussing with an experienced tax accountant.

Rule 4: Not Lavish or Extravagant

The expenses must not be lavish or extravagant under the circumstances. Defining what is or is not lavish or extravagant under the circumstances depends on, well, depends on the circumstances.

The bigger the business and the more income the business earns, the more likely you can deduct large amounts of money and call the expenses "not lavish or extravagant under the circumstances." Full-time, ongoing businesses can usually get away with a bit more lavishness than part-time and new businesses. But there are no specific rules. My own guideline: If you think a deduction might be considered lavish or extravagant, there is a good likelihood that it is. This is an area where I suggest you talk to an experienced tax accountant.

There is no question that all four basic requirements are sometimes vague and subject to interpretation. The IRS, fortunately, tends to be quite reasonable about what's reasonable ("not lavish or extravagant"), as well as what is ordinary and necessary. If the expense is business related, if it isn't outrageously extravagant, if it doesn't stick out on your tax return like a tuba in a string quartet, you are probably okay.

And remember, try to get receipts for everything—and keep them.

And One More . . . The $27 Million Dollar Rule

Businesses with income of $27 million or more have different rules for several tax deductions listed in this book. (Businesses with income of $27 million or more have different rules for most everything.)

If this is you, give this book to some aspiring entrepreneur and hire yourself a team of aggressive powerhouse attorneys, and maybe a lobbyist or two.

4

475 Tax Deductions, A to Z

Tax laws are steeped in complexity. And we have gone from complexity to perplexity.

—Former IRS Commissioner Doug Shulman

From Accountants to Zoning, these 475 listings are arranged in alphabetical order. Deductions that may not be obvious are defined and explained. Special situations—such as rules for home businesses, manufacturers, corporations, employers, or specific kinds of businesses—are labeled in bold and explained.

This alphabetical listing also includes tax credits, which are different than tax deductions, as explained in chapter 2; and business expenses that are not deductible, just so you'll know.

Some of the subheadings in the listing:

Expense category. The expense category suggests where to put the deduction on your tax form. However, as mentioned in chapter 1, many deductions could easily come under different expense categories. Which category you choose is often not important. What *is* important is being sure you take the deduction, regardless of the category.

New businesses. Expenses associated with buying a business and expenses incurred before starting your business come under special rules. Tax deductions are limited. As soon as you start operating your business, these startup limitations no longer apply. See Buying a Business, Startup Costs, and, if you are starting a corporation, Organizational Costs.

Home-Based Business. Almost every tax deduction listed in this book applies to home-based businesses. The few tax deductions that are different for home-based businesses are flagged. Look for the bold **Home-Based Business** at the end of an entry.

Most of the differences between home-based businesses and other businesses have to do with deducting the business portion of the home itself. Read the Home Expenses entry. Any business owner who uses part of his or her home for business purposes, whether the business is home based or not, may be eligible for the Home Expenses deduction.

IRS Red Flag Audit Warning. Some tax deductions, especially ones that could easily be for nonbusiness expenses—fun stuff like going out to dinner, traveling, or flying your airplane—are always on the IRS radar as suspicious. The expenses might be legitimate business expenses, legally deductible, but IRS auditors are not the most trusting people, and they are always on the lookout for these "red flags," especially if the deductions are large. Sometimes, especially if the tax savings is small, it might be better not to take a deduction that could invite an audit.

More information. If you want to learn more about specific tax deductions, the IRS publishes dozens of tax booklets, which they update every year. All the IRS publications are free, available as print editions or as PDF downloads. View, download, or order print publications from IRS.gov or call (800) 829-3676. Two IRS publications useful to all businesses are Publication 334, *Tax Guide for Small Business*, and Publication 535, *Business Expenses*.

Napoleon Bonaparte waged war. Britain had to raise money for defense, so levied the first English income tax. It set a pattern for income taxes elsewhere. Burning hatred of Napoleon lives on to this day.

—L. M. Boyd, "Grab Bag,"
San Francisco Chronicle

Accountants

It figures that the very first entry would be Accountants. Accountants' fees are deductible.

Business consultations with an accountant are deductible. Accounting, bookkeeping, payroll, tax return preparation, auditing, tax advice, and similar services are all deductible. The cost of hiring an accountant to help you with an IRS audit is deductible.

For preparing the tax return of a sole proprietor or a one-person LLC, only the cost of preparing the business part of the 1040 tax return (Schedule C and related schedules) is deductible as a business expense. Ask your accountant to separate out the fee for the business and personal parts of your tax return, or just prorate the cost yourself. Unless you have a lot of nonbusiness tax issues, I'd figure that 90% of the cost is business related.

Expense category: Legal and Professional Services.

Accounting software: Accounting and tax software that you lease or subscribe to can be deducted currently. Software that you purchase can be deducted currently, or it can be amortized over three years; see Software.

Expense category: For leased or subscribed software, Office Expenses. For purchased software, Other Expenses.

A tax is a compulsory payment for which no specific benefit is received.

—U.S. Treasury

Accident Insurance

Insurance covering accidents is deductible but as part of other types of insurance.

Vehicle accident insurance comes under the tax deduction rules for vehicles. See Vehicles. Accident insurance that is part of a health insurance policy is deducted under the rules for health insurance. See Health Insurance. Workers' compensation insurance that covers you if you are injured at work is deductible only if your state requires you to have the coverage, which most states don't require unless you are an employee of your own corporation. See Workers' Compensation Insurance.

Expense category: Depends on what kind of insurance you purchase.

(Yes, I know, Accident should come before Accountants, but I did not want to start the book with an accident.)

ADA Expenses

Costs of complying with the Americans with Disabilities Act can be deducted under a variety of rules. See Disabled Access.

Advances

Advances paid to contractors, professionals, vendors and suppliers are deductible.

Expense category: Varies depending on actual expenses.

Prepayments: If the advance is a prepayment for goods or services to be received in the following year—if, for example, you pay in December for goods to be delivered or work to be done in January—the deduction may have to be postponed to next year. Some prepayments can be deducted currently, but some prepayments cannot be deducted until the following year. The IRS has a specific list of what is and isn't currently deductible. See Prepayments.

Refunds: If an advance is later refunded to you, and if you've already taken a deduction for it, you reduce your current expenses or increase your gross income by the amount of the refund. Either way, the net effect is the same: to reverse the deduction you originally claimed.

Deposits and down payments: Some advances are called deposits or down payments, but they are not always the same thing. Generally, refundable deposits are not deductible. Nonrefundable deposits are deductible. But like advances, deposits and down payments that are actually prepayments of some expense come under the prepaid expense rules. See Prepayments.

Paying yourself: Self-employed individuals cannot deduct any advances you pay to yourself. See Paying Yourself.

Employers: Advances to employees are wages, taxable to the employees and deductible for the employer at the time the advance is given. See Wages.

Corporations: Owners of corporations are employees of their businesses. Advances to yourself are taxable employee wages. The rules are the same as the rules for employers.

And it came to pass in those days that there went out a decree from Caesar Augustus, that all the world should be taxed. This decree seems to have been enforced ever since.

—Professor C. Northcote Parkinson

Advertising

Advertising is deductible.

Advertising is a very broad category and includes most expenses that promote or bring recognition to your business. Ads, flyers, catalogs, and sponsorships are deductible. Giveaways such as pens or souvenirs with your business name or logo are deductible. Contests and prizes are deductible, but see Prizes for an important tax issue.

Expense category: Advertising.

Political prohibition: You cannot deduct the cost of advertising in political programs or at political events or meetings.

Donations: Donations you make to charities and community organizations that help promote your business are sometimes deductible as advertising expenses, depending on what you donate. See Donations.

Agents

For musicians and entertainers, booking agents usually deduct their fees from whatever pay is coming to you, so there is no additional deduction.

But if you pay any booking fees, or any other fees out of your pocket, the fees are deductible.

Expense category: Commissions and Fees.

Agricultural Businesses

See Farming.

Air-Conditioning

Portable air conditioners can be deducted the year purchased and first used in the business, or at your option, depreciated over seven years. For details and special situations, see Business Assets.

Expense category: Depreciation or Other Expenses, depending on several factors. See Business Assets.

Built-in: Built-in air-conditioning can be deducted the year purchased and installed, or at your option, depreciated over several years: the life of the building if you own the building, fifteen years if you are leasing the building. See Building Improvements.

Home-Based Business: A portable air conditioner for the business portion of the home can be deducted or depreciated. Built-in air-conditioning is part of the Home Expenses deduction, not deducted separately. See Home Expenses.

---

*In seventeen hundred seventy six, a group of American mavericks
Renounced the yoke of tyranny, the tax on stamps the tax on tea
Our fathers felt that we were fit, to tax ourselves and you'll admit
We have been very good at it.*

—American lyricist Howard Dietz (1896–1983)

Aircraft

Business aircraft can be deducted the year purchased and first used in the business, or at your option, depreciated over five years. For details and special situations, see Business Assets.

If aircraft is used partly for nonbusiness purposes, the costs are prorated between business and personal use.

The cost to rent, lease, or charter an aircraft for business can be deducted.

Expense category: If rented or leased, Rental Expense. If purchased, Depreciation or Other Expenses, depending on several factors. See Business Assets.

Employers: If any of your employees use your business's aircraft for personal trips (not business related), the value of the flights is considered taxable wages subject to all payroll taxes.

Corporations: Owners of corporations are employees of their businesses. The rules for employees also apply to owner-employees of the corporation.

IRS Red Flag Audit Warning: Unless you are in the airplane business—flying, leasing, servicing, selling—a business deduction for owning or using aircraft could increase your likelihood of an audit. Flying around in the corporate jet and deducting the expenses may be pushing the envelope, as the hotshot pilots say. If you are audited, the IRS will ask to see detailed records of the aircraft's use, looking for invalid deductions that were in fact personal, nonbusiness expenses.

Airfare

Deductible if certain requirements are met. See Travel.

Alarms

Alarm systems can be deducted the year purchased and first used in the business, or at your option, depreciated over fifteen years. For details and special situations, see Business Assets.

Monthly service charges and alarm rentals are fully deductible.

Expense category: If rented or leased, Rent or Lease. If purchased, Depreciation or Other Expenses, depending on several factors. See Business Assets. Service charges, Office Expenses.

Home-Based Business: Alarm systems in your home are part of the Home Expenses deduction, not deducted separately. See Home Expenses.

Allowance for Bad Debts

An allowance for bad debts, funds set aside in anticipation of a bad debt, is not deductible. Actual bad debts may or may not be deductible. See Bad Debts.

Americans with Disabilities Act

See Disabled Access.

Amortization

Intangible assets such as trademarks and patents are deducted over a period of years. The deduction is called amortization. It is similar to depreciation. The procedure is the same and the tax deduction rules are the same. See Depreciation.
  Expense category: Other Expenses.
  Trademark license: If you acquire rights to a trademark from another business under a licensing agreement, the payments are deductible when paid. They do not have to be amortized. *Expense category:* Other Expenses.
  Loan amortization: The term *amortization* also refers to paying off a loan. Loan amortization is not a deductible expense. A loan is not income when you get it and is not an expense when you pay it off. Any interest is deductible. See Interest.

Animals

A tax accountant I know has a large brass plaque on his desk that says, "Don't invest in anything that eats." But since you did anyway, the cost of purchasing and maintaining any animal that meets the IRS ordinary and necessary tests can be deducted.
  A watchdog or guard dog meets these tests. See Guard Dog. Farm animals come under rules for farmers. See Farming. Animal breeders treat the cost of their animals as inventory. See Inventory.
  Animal businesses: Businesses that board, groom, or train animals can deduct their animal-related expenses like any other business expenses, depending on what the expenses are actually for.

Answering Machine

Answering machine? An answering machine, if you still use one, can be deducted the year purchased and first used in the business, or at your option, depreciated over five years. For details and special situations, see Business Assets.

Expense category: Depreciation or Other Expenses, depending on several factors. See Business Assets.

Answering Service

Telephone answering service fees are deductible. Any initial setup or installation charges are also deductible.

Expense category: Legal and Professional Services.

If Patrick Henry thought that taxation without representation was bad, he should see how bad it is with representation.

—Farmer's Almanac

Antiques

Valuable antiques, if used for decoration only, cannot be depreciated and cannot be deducted until sold. Antiques actually used in the business, such as an old desk or a professional musician's rare instrument, come under conflicting rules.

The IRS has always said that rare and valuable antiques cannot be depreciated or written off, regardless of how they are used. The Tax Court has overruled the IRS on several occasions and allowed the deduction if the item being deducted can wear out or deteriorate from use (which applies to just about everything except maybe Fred Flintstone's granite desk).

I do not know how the IRS determines if something is rare and valuable or even if it is an antique, a term with no legal definition. If it were me, I would assume that my beautiful oak filing cabinet was old, but not *that* old, and take the deduction. Like too many IRS laws, it's a judgment call.

If you choose to take the deduction, you can write off your antique whatever-it-is the year purchased and first used in the business, or at your option, depreciate it over seven years. See Business Assets.

Expense category: Depreciation or Other Expenses, depending on several factors. See Business Assets.

Dealers in antiques: Treat antiques as inventory. The IRS prohibition does not apply to you. See Inventory.

Appraisal Fees

Appraisal fees paid to determine the amount of a loss are deductible. Real estate appraisal fees are deductible. Appraisal fees involving the purchase or sale of a business may have to be capitalized (deducted over several years); see Startup Costs.

Expense category: Legal and Professional Services.

Apps

Business-related apps (originally called application software) that you pay for or subscribe to are deductible.

Expense category: Office Expenses.

Software designers: If you design or develop apps, you are allowed the same deductions as software developers. See Software.

Art Treasures

The IRS says that art treasures do not depreciate in value, so no deduction or depreciation is allowed. The IRS does not define art treasure, but a business that purchases and writes off very expensive art may find the IRS objecting. The IRS says that you report a profit or loss on art treasures when you sell them.

Dealers in art: Treat art as inventory. The prohibition on deducting art treasures does not apply to you. See Inventory.

Artwork

Office decorations can be deducted the year purchased and first used in the business, or at your option, depreciated over seven years. For details and special situations, see Business Assets.

Expense category: Depreciation or Other Expenses, depending on several factors. See Business Assets.

Assessments

Local government assessments for repair (not construction) of streets, sidewalks, water lines, sewers, and the like are deductible.

Expense category: Taxes and Licenses.

Assessments for improvements to your property are not deductible. The expense is added to the cost of your property and depreciated. These assessments include new construction of streets, sidewalks, and water and sewer lines. See Depreciation.

Expense category: Depreciation.

More information: IRS Publication 946, *How to Depreciate Property.*

Home-Based Business: Property assessments are part of the Home Expenses deduction, not deducted separately. See Home Expenses.

Assets

Business assets can be deducted the year of purchase or depreciated over several years. See Business Assets.

Americans have the impression that understanding the tax laws will only serve to increase the amount of taxes they must pay.

—Mike Mares, American Institute of Certified Public Accountants

---

Associations

Dues and other expenses for professional organizations, merchant and trade associations, business leagues, unions, chambers of commerce, and similar business groups are deductible. Dues to community service organizations such as Rotary, Lions, and Kiwanis are deductible.

Expense category: Other Expenses.

Political: If part of your dues to an association or a union is for political lobbying, that portion of the dues is not deductible.

Clubs: Dues and membership fees in clubs, including business clubs, are not deductible.

Meetings and seminars: The cost of attending business meetings and seminars is deductible even if held at a club or other nonbusiness location. See Travel.

Athletic Facilities

Dues and membership fees to athletic clubs are not deductible.

Athletic and recreation facilities on the business premises are deductible if they are open to all employees. For structures and built-in structural components, see Building Improvements. For equipment, see Business Assets.

Expense category: Depends on what is being deducted.

IRS Red Flag Audit Warning: Unless you have a lot of employees and a big operation, any deduction for athletic facilities or equipment could invite an audit.

ATM Fees

ATM (automatic teller machine) fees are deductible.

Expense category: Office Expenses or Other Expenses.

The hardest thing in the world to understand is income tax.

—Albert Einstein

Attorneys

I met with an attorney once and asked him what he charged. He said he charged $400 to answer three questions. I laughed and asked him if he was joking. He said no, he wasn't joking. Then he asked me what my third question was.

Attorney fees are deductible, but see two exceptions below. Also see Lawsuits.

Expense category: Legal and Professional Services.

Exceptions: Expenses incurred before starting your business and expenses associated with buying a business come under special rules. See Buying a Business, Startup Costs, and, if you are starting a corporation, Organizational Costs. Attorney fees related to acquiring property may have to be capitalized, added to the cost of the property. If this is a substantial sum, I suggest talking to an experienced accountant.

This has nothing to do with this deduction, but most small businesses do not usually need to hire an attorney. Most business issues, including many legal requirements, can be handled by an experienced accountant who probably charges less than an attorney. A good accountant will know when an attorney is required.

Audits

The cost of an audit by an accountant or some other professional is deductible. The cost of hiring an accountant or lawyer to defend yourself in an IRS audit of your business is deductible. Any taxes or IRS penalties are not deductible.

Expense category: Legal and Professional Services.

Under an IRS pilot program, companies will have a chance to volunteer for IRS audits.

—Kiplinger Tax Letter

Helping the IRS improve the audit process is like a mouse helping to build a better mousetrap.

—Paul Gada, CCH Tax Publications

A fool and his money are soon parted.

—Thomas Tusser, British farmer (1524–1580)

Automobiles

You can deduct the cost of using an automobile for business, or you can take the Standard Mileage Rate. See Vehicles.

Awards

For awards and prizes given out to customers, see Prizes.

Employers: Awards paid to employees are considered taxable wages subject to all payroll taxes. It does not matter if an award is money, debit card, gift certificate, or goods: the awards are taxable. However, small token awards of merchandise, but not cash or gift cards or gift certificates, are not taxable to the employee.

There is one exception to the employee award rule. The IRS recognizes something they call an employee achievement award. Employee achievement awards are for length of service or for safety, but not for things like top salesperson of the month or extra hours worked. Employee achievement awards cannot be "disguised compensation."

Up to $400 per year in merchandise (but not cash or cash equivalents such as gift cards) can be given to an employee tax free as an employee achievement award, and you, the employer, get a tax deduction. The maximum increases to $1,600 a year per employee if you have a qualified plan, a written awards policy that meets certain IRS requirements. A good accountant should be able to help you create a qualified plan.

Expense category: Employee Benefit Programs.

There is something un-American about a tax system that cannot be understood by an intelligent American.

—Tax expert and Stanford University professor George Marotta

Babysitting

See Dependent Care.

Bad Debts

Some bad debts are deductible, some are not.

Deductible bad debts include customers' bounced checks and credit card charges customers refuse to pay: payments you received and posted to your income record before you found out the check or credit card was no good.

If a customer owes you money but never pays, you cannot take a bad debt expense for uncollectible accounts (if you use the cash method of accounting, which most small businesses use) because the income was not recorded in the first place. You get a bad debt deduction only if you recorded income in your income ledger that you are unable to collect.

A self-employed individual cannot take a bad debt deduction for his or her own time devoted to a client or customer who doesn't pay. You do not get a deduction for the income you should have earned, the money you were cheated out of. I know that doesn't sound fair, and it isn't, but that is how the tax laws are written. You are out the money you should have earned, and the IRS says, Tough luck.

You do get a deduction for any inventory (goods) you sold that you didn't get paid for. See Inventory.

Deduct only those bad debts you are certain are uncollectible. Each bad debt should be specifically identified. Amounts cannot be estimated. If you are unsure, you can wait until next year. You can write off a bad debt in any future year that it becomes definitely uncollectible.

Expense category: Bad Debts.

Bad debt reserve: A few businesses that anticipate large bad debts sometimes set aside money in a bad debt reserve fund, sort of like self-insurance. Such reserves are not really business expenses and are not tax deductible.

Bank Charges

Bank charges, services, ATM fees, penalties, and check or credit card fees are deductible. Credit card chargebacks are deductible. Check printing costs are deductible.

Expense category: Office Expenses.

Bankruptcy

Cost of filing for bankruptcy and related expenses are deductible.
Expense category: Legal and Professional Services.

Customer bankruptcy: If one of your customers files for bankruptcy and you are unable to collect money owed to you, you cannot take a bad debt expense for uncollectible accounts (if you use the cash method of accounting, which most small businesses use) because the income was not recorded in the first place. You get a bad debt deduction only if you recorded income in your income ledger that you are unable to collect. Any expenses you incur to try to collect the debts are deductible.

Supplier bankruptcy: If a supplier goes bankrupt, and if you have paid for goods or services not delivered, you can deduct your loss as a bad debt.
Expense category: Bad Debts.

Barter/Trade

Business-related goods or services acquired by barter or trade (the same thing) are tax deductible. The amount you deduct is the fair market value of what you receive, what you would have normally paid for the goods or services had you been paying cash.

Expense category: Depends on what is acquired in trade.

IRS Red Flag Audit Warning: The IRS does not like barter transactions because barter income is too easy to hide. In IRS audits of businesses, one of the first questions often asked is, Do you engage in trade or barter? A yes answer is a signal to the auditor to expand the scope of the audit, looking for unreported income.

Barter income: Be aware that the fair market value of the goods or services you receive in a barter transaction is taxable income, included in your regular business income and treated just like any other business income. It does not matter what you receive or how you use it. It could be a business computer or a paint job for your office, or it could be a guitar or horse-riding lessons for your kid. Either way, the value of what you receive is taxable business income. But you only get a tax deduction if what you receive is for your business.

Barter club/exchange: If you join a barter club or exchange, the rules are basically the same. Barter club commissions and fees are deductible if the transaction is for your business. Barter clubs report all transactions to the IRS.

Cryptocurrency: Businesses that deal in cryptocurrency such as bitcoins are conducting business identical to barter transactions as far as the IRS and tax law are concerned. The amount you record as an expense is the fair market value of the goods or services received.

Benefits

For employee fringe benefits, see Fringe Benefits. For other benefits, look up the individual items.

Bicycles

Bicycles used for business can be deducted the year purchased and first used in the business, or at your option, depreciated over seven years. For details and special situations, see Business Assets.

If the bicycle is used partly for nonbusiness purposes, the costs are prorated between business and personal use.

Expense category: Depreciation or Other Expenses, depending on several factors. See Business Assets.

All the Congress, all the accountants and tax lawyers, all the judges, cannot tell for sure what the income tax law says.

—Former Citicorp Chairman Walter B. Wriston

Billboards

Rental costs for billboards are deductible.

Billboards you own can be deducted the year purchased and first used in the business, or at your option, depreciated over fifteen years. For details and special situations, see Business Assets.

Expense category: If renting or leasing, Rent or Lease. If purchasing, Depreciation or Other Expenses, depending on several factors. See Business Assets.

Bitcoins

See Cryptocurrency.

Blue Sky

Blue sky is another term for goodwill, an intangible asset. If purchased as part of the purchase price of a business, it is amortized over fifteen years. See Goodwill. Also see Buying a Business.

Expense category: Other Expenses.

Blue sky laws mean something different than blue sky. *Blue sky laws* is (are?) a general term for state laws that regulate investments, originally an attempt to stop real estate fraud. The terms *blue sky laws* and *blue sky* both come from the monetary worth of the blue sky above—that is, nothing—which is what too many unregulated investments were worth. And what some people also think goodwill is worth.

In one way, the Tax Code is the great equalizer. Nobody understands it.

—Rev. L. C. Lewis, Willits, California

Boats

If needed for business, boats and other watercraft can be deducted the year purchased and first used in the business, or at your option, depreciated over ten years. For details and special situations, see Business Assets.

Boats used for recreation are usually not deductible even if they are used only for business purposes.

Expense category: Depreciation or Other Expenses, depending on several factors. See Business Assets.

IRS Red Flag Audit Warning: Unless you are in the business of operating boats (fishing, charters, rentals, tugboat, or other marine-related business), a business deduction for any kind of watercraft will increase your likelihood of an audit. If audited, the IRS may ask to see detailed records of the boat's use, looking for invalid deductions that were in fact personal, nonbusiness expenses.

Bodyguard

(1) If needing a bodyguard is an ordinary and necessary expense of your business, it is a deductible expense. (2) If needing a bodyguard is an ordinary and necessary expense of your business, I would suggest you start a different business.

Expense category: Other Expenses.

Bonds

There are different kinds of bonds with different deduction rules.

Surety bonds: A surety bond is a type of insurance. If you do not complete a job, for any reason, a surety bond pays the costs. Service businesses such as auto repair shops and building contractors are often required by law to have surety bonds. The cost of surety bonds is deductible.

Expense category: Insurance.

Fidelity bonds: A fidelity bond is also a type of insurance. Fidelity bonds are placed on employees, insuring against theft or embezzlement by the bonded employees. If you have employees going into people's homes and businesses, such as a janitorial service, a fidelity bond protects you and the client should one of your employees turn out to be a thief. You can also have fidelity bonds on independent contractors you hire. The cost of fidelity bonds is deductible.

Expense category: Insurance.

Interest-bearing bonds: There are monetary documents called bonds, interest-bearing "instruments" as they are often called, similar to notes or loans. The bonds themselves are not deductible. The interest is deductible.

Expense category: Interest.

Bonus

Self-employed individuals cannot deduct any bonus you pay to yourself. See Paying Yourself.

Employers: Bonuses given to employees are wages, taxable to the employees and deductible for the employer at the time the bonus is given. Year-end bonuses are deducted the year the bonus is given. A bonus handed out in January for the previous December is a January expense, deductible in the new year. See Wages.

Corporations: Owners of corporations are employees of their businesses. Bonuses you pay to yourself are taxable employee wages. The rules are the same as the rules for employers.

Booking Agency Fees

For musicians and entertainers, booking agents usually deduct their fees from whatever pay is coming to you, so there is no additional deduction. But if you pay any booking fees, or any other fees out of your pocket, the fees are deductible.
Expense category: Commissions and Fees.

Bookkeeping

Bookkeeping, recordkeeping, accounting, and similar services are deductible. Cloud or other internet-based software can be deducted currently. Bookkeeping software you purchase can be deducted currently or can be amortized over three years; see Software.
Expense category: For services, Legal and Professional Services. For internet subscriptions or access, Office Expenses. For software purchased, Other Expenses.
Also see Accountants.

Lots of things can happen if you don't keep the right records, and none of them are good.

—CPA Dan Smogor

Books

Books, magazines, newsletters, newspapers, and all other publications are deductible. The cost of buying and maintaining your books (your financial records) is deductible.
Expense category: For publications, Office Expenses. For bookkeeping services, Legal and Professional Services.

Bounced Checks

Bounced checks are deductible, the ones your lousy customers bounce on you. You can deduct the amount of the check, assuming you recorded the check as income when you got the check. Any bank charges are also deductible.

Expense category: For the amount of the check, Bad Debts. For the bank charge, Office Expenses.

Your own bounced checks, the ones you wrote, are not deductible. Because nothing was actually paid, right? That makes sense, doesn't it? Bank charges and penalties are deductible.

Boxes

Boxes, cartons, and other containers and packaging materials that hold the goods you sell are considered part of your inventory. See Inventory.

If, however, the cost of the boxes is not significant or if the boxes are used only occasionally, most businesses deduct the costs currently as shipping supplies.

Expense category: Supplies.

Bribes

Bribes that are legal and that meet the IRS's ordinary and necessary tests are deductible. Illegal bribes are not deductible.

It is illegal to bribe a U.S. or foreign government official, to offer a bribe to win a foreign contract, to bribe a contractor working on a federally funded project, or to bribe a banker to influence loan transactions. Illegal payments are not deductible.

Some bribes are legal, and legal bribes are deductible. The federal government has no laws against bribing a company official, a purchasing agent, a sales rep, or other people not involved with the government or banking. But your state may outlaw these bribes. If the bribe is illegal in your state, no deduction. The IRS goes by state laws on this deduction.

Expense category: If legal, Other Expenses.

Also see Kickbacks. Or not. You can run a successful business without ever resorting to underhanded or questionable or distasteful transactions. Stand tall and, as Jiminy Cricket said, Always let your conscience be your guide.

Broker's Fees

A broker's fee to buy or sell real estate is added to the value of the real estate and depreciated. See Buildings. A broker's fee for buying or selling a business is amortized over five years. See Buying a Business.

Any other broker's fees paid in the normal course of business are deductible.

Expense category: Legal and Professional Services.

Building Components

Most building components are considered part of the building and are depreciated along with the building. See Buildings.

Some components of buildings, however, can be depreciated separately from, and at a faster rate than, the building itself. Movable partitions, built-in supports for heavy equipment, portable air-conditioning, awnings, and some fixtures may fall into this category. See Building Improvements below.

There is a big gap between what the IRS permits and what companies do in practice.

—U.S. Chamber of Commerce

Building Improvements

Many building improvements, renovations, remodeling, refreshing, and repairs—all somewhat overlapping terms—can be deducted currently, but some building improvements are depreciated over several years, depending on several factors.

The general rule for building improvements, though with several exceptions, is that improvements that add to the value or extend the useful life of a building or adapt the building to a new use are depreciated over the life of the building. The exceptions:

Improvements of $2,500 or less: Under a law called de minimis safe harbor, any improvements of $2,500 or less can be deducted currently. The terms *de minimis* and *safe harbor* are explained under Business Assets, which I encourage you to read.

Improvements of $10,000 or less: Another IRS safe harbor rule, known as Safe Harbor for Small Taxpayers, can be used by any business that has annual gross sales of $10 million or less (the IRS's definition of a "small" taxpayer) and applies to any building that costs $1 million or less. You can deduct up to $10,000 a year in building improvements and repairs, but only up to a maximum of 2% of the building's cost. So for a building that costs under $500,000, the maximum you can deduct for improvements and repairs is 2% of the cost of the building. Improvement costs greater than the 2% maximum are depreciated over the life of the building. This rule applies to buildings you own or are renting.

Improvements to retail stores and restaurants: Under a law called Remodel-Refresh Safe Harbor, owners of retail stores and restaurants can deduct 75% of the cost of remodeling and depreciate the 25% balance over fifteen years. You can ignore this 75%–25% rule, and take a full deduction currently, for improvements that meet the $2,500 or $10,000 rules above.

Leasehold improvements: Leasehold improvements are nonstructural components of a building that you are renting or leasing, such as air-conditioning, fixtures, support for heavy machinery, partitions, and awnings.

If you, the tenant, are paying for leasehold improvements, you can deduct the expenses that meet any of the exceptions under Building Improvements above. Expenditures that don't meet the above exceptions can be depreciated over fifteen years.

Repairs: The IRS laws for deducting repairs are contradictory and confusing (and explained under Repairs), but the bottom line is that most small businesses can deduct any repairs costing $10,000 or less. Repairs come under the two "safe harbor" rules explained above.

Depreciation as an option: Improvements that are eligible to be deducted currently can instead, at your option, be depreciated, deducting some of the expense this year and some of the expense in future years. Most businesses prefer whenever possible to take the current deduction (writing off the entire expense) because the calculations are simple and the tax savings are immediate. For more information on depreciation and why you might want to take it instead of deducting the entire expense currently, see Depreciation.

Expense category: If deducting under the safe harbor rules, Other Expenses. If deducting as a repair, Repairs and Maintenance. If depreciating, Depreciation.

More information: For depreciation, IRS Publication 946, *How to Depreciate Property*. For the safe harbor de minimis deduction, IRS Notice 2015-82, *De Minimis Safe Harbor Deduction*.

Home-Based Business: Home renovations and repairs are part of the Home Expenses deduction, not deducted separately. See Home Expenses.

The only thing that hurts more than having to pay income tax is not having to pay income tax.

—Sir Thomas R. Dewar, founder, Dewar's Scottish Whiskey

Buildings

Lease or rent on buildings used for business is deductible. See Leases and Rents. Buildings that you own are depreciated, with some exceptions noted below. See Depreciation.

Deductible buildings: Some bulk storage facilities, single-purpose agricultural and horticultural buildings, restaurant property, retail property, and some energy-saving improvements to commercial real estate can be deducted the year of purchase.

Expense category: If owned, Depreciation. If renting or leasing, Rent or Lease.

More information: IRS Publication 946, *How to Depreciate Property.*

Building improvements: Building improvements, remodeling, or renovating can be deducted currently or depreciated, depending on several factors. See Building Improvements.

Renting to yourself: A sole proprietor who owns a building cannot rent the building to his or her business. For tax purposes, there is no rental income or rental expense. The owner of a corporation can rent a building to his or her corporation, and the corporation can get a tax deduction, but the rent would be taxable income to the owner of the corporation. Likewise, partners can rent buildings to the partnership, though there can be tax complications in such an arrangement. This is an area to discuss with an experienced accountant. Who legally owns the building, you or your business, and how you structure the deduction can have a major impact on taxes.

Land: The land under the building cannot be depreciated or deducted. You get no tax deduction until you sell the land. For depreciation deductions, you will need to separate the cost of the building from the cost of the land.

Rehabilitation Tax Credit: If you are rehabilitating a certified historic building for use in your business, you may be eligible for this tax credit. See Tax Credits.

Disabled Access Tax Credit: If you renovate your workplace to accommodate people with disabilities, you may be eligible for this tax credit. See Disabled Access.

Real estate developers: Predevelopment costs such as planning and design, blueprints, building permits, engineering studies, landscape plans, and the like cannot be deducted currently but have to be capitalized. If you construct low-income housing, you may be eligible for a Low-Income Housing Tax Credit. See Tax Credits.

Home-Based Business: Buildings are part of the Home Expenses deduction, not deducted separately. See Home Expenses.

Burglary

See Casualty Losses.

Bus

You can deduct the cost of using a bus for business, but with limitations. See Vehicles.

Mobile businesses and touring entertainers: If you are staying in a bus while traveling, your travel and living expenses are deductible, and the cost of meals is 50% deductible. If, however, you are constantly traveling, living in your bus, the IRS considers the bus to be your home and will disallow most travel expenses, including the costs of operating the bus. This is a major issue with IRS auditors. See Travel.

Business Assets

Most tangible business assets, both new and used (other than buildings) can be deducted the year you purchase the asset, or, at your option, can be depreciated over several years.

Business assets are possessions that you own and use in your business (not renting): machinery, equipment, tools, furniture, fixtures, office machines, computers, display cases, vehicles, and assets specific to the kind of business or profession you're in such as a musician's instruments or a surveyor's transit.

Some assets do not come under the rules for business assets: Buildings. Intangible assets such as patents, trademarks, and copyrights. Software. Land. Valuable antiques. Inventory. Supplies and inexpensive assets that are used up or wear out in a year or less. Any assets you are renting or leasing. Look up each item to find out about deductions.

Deducting versus depreciating: Most businesses deduct the full cost of assets the year of purchase, but that may not be the best option for tax savings. Before taking this deduction, read the Depreciation entry to find out if depreciation may be a better choice.

If you do choose to deduct the full cost of an asset (instead of depreciation), the IRS has two options for writing off tangible assets the year you purchase them, and a third option allowing a partial write-off.

The different option have different rules, depending on how much the assets cost. These options are often overlapping, and confusing, the result of different laws passed at different times without any of the law writers paying attention to what was already on the books.

OPTION 1: Assets that cost $2,500 or less can be deducted the year you purchase them, with no restrictions. The limit increases to $5,000 per asset if your business has what's called an Applicable Financial Statement, or AFS, which means you've gone through a CPA audit, which few if any small businesses have done.

This option is called the De Minimis Safe Harbor Method. *De minimis* means trivial or insignificant, which I sure wouldn't call $2,500, but then the IRS and I live in different worlds. It's called "safe harbor" because the IRS decided that $2,500 was too small an amount to waste their time on, so they won't question you, you're "safe" to take the deduction. If you choose this option, you must use it for all tangible assets that cost $2,500 or less.

Assets that cost $2,500 or less can be deducted under Option 2 instead of Option 1, though there are maximum limits under Option 2.

Expense category: Other Expenses. You are also required to include a statement with your tax return listing the assets individually.

More information: IRS Notice 2015-82, *De Minimis Safe Harbor Deduction.*

OPTION 2: Most assets (regardless of cost) other than buildings can be deducted the year you purchase them, but with restrictions.

This option can be used for most personal assets, including the $2,500-or-less assets that are eligible for Option 1. But this option, known as the First-Year Write-Off or Section 179 Deduction, has an annual maximum and other restrictions that Option 1 does not. If any of the restriction apply to your business, you are better off using Option 1 for the $2,500 assets and using this option for the more expensive assets.

Taxable income limit: The deduction cannot exceed your taxable income. For sole proprietors, taxable income is all income, both business and nonbusiness, reported on your tax return (married couples combined if filing jointly). Any deduction disallowed because of this income limitation can be carried forward to the next year, and future years if necessary, until the assets are fully written off.

Maximum deduction: This option has an annual maximum deduction of $1,160,000 all assets combined. Assets that exceed the maximum are depreciated. If you have more than one unincorporated business, or a husband and wife each have a separate business, the maximum is for all of the businesses combined. The maximum is reduced if you purchase more than $2,890,000 in depreciable assets in any one year.

Other restrictions: Assets used 50% or less for business, and assets owned before going into business, are not eligible. Automobiles and SUVs have a lower maximum Section 179 Deduction.

Expense category: Depreciation.

More information: IRS Publication 946, *How to Depreciate Property.*

OPTION 3: A partial write-off of business assets. A percentage of the cost of tangible assets (except for most buildings) can be deducted the year purchased under a law called Bonus Depreciation. The balance of the cost is depreciated, so this is not an option for anyone wanting a 100% deduction the first year.

Option 3 expires after 2026. For 2023, the maximum bonus depreciation deduction was 80%. It drops to 60% in 2024, 40% in 2025, and 20% in 2026. The deduction is eliminated starting 2027. See Depreciation.

Additional rules for all three options:

Maximum deduction: The deduction for business assets cannot exceed the net profit from the business. Costs not deductible in any one year can, in some situations, be carried forward to future years.

Year of purchase versus first use: If you buy an asset one year but don't take delivery until the next year, or if you buy and receive an asset one year but don't use it until the next year, you may or may not be able to deduct the purchase until the following year. I highly suggest (1) make sure you receive and use an asset the year you pay for it, and if you didn't (2) talk to an experienced accountant to figure out what you can or cannot deduct.

Installment purchases: Assets purchased in installments with payments over more than one year can be written off the year you first use the assets.

Selling an asset: If you sell assets you've previously written off, or convert them to nonbusiness use, you may have to "recapture" the amount you wrote off (add it back into income), depending on how many years you own the assets.

Disabled Access Credit: Equipment that is used to assist disabled employees or customers is eligible for the Disabled Access Tax Credit. See Disabled Access.

Dealers in business assets: Companies that sell business assets, such as office supply stores, furniture stores, equipment dealers, and car dealerships, and companies that manufacture business assets treat the assets they sell as inventory. The business asset rules above do not apply to these businesses (for the assets they manufacture or sell).

Business Associations

Most expenses for business associations are deductible. See Associations.

Business Cards

Business cards are deductible.
   Expense category: Office Expenses.

Business Gifts

Tax deductions for business gifts are limited to $25 per recipient in any one year. Now that's one generous tax deduction, $25. What's amazing is that the $25 maximum has been unchanged for over 40 years. I have an old tax book from 1976 that mentions the same $25 maximum.
   Exceptions: There are a few exceptions to the $25 maximum. Gifts with your company name or logo imprinted on them are exempt from the $25 limitation. Gifts to business entities, such as a gift to a corporation, if not given to specific individuals, are exempt from the limitation.
   Prizes awarded to customers are not business gifts and are not subject to the $25 limitation, but prizes have tax problems you should know about. See Prizes.
   Samples of your merchandise, given to prospective buyers or to people who might review or publicize your products, are not considered gifts and are not subject to the gift limitation. You write off the cost of the free samples (not the retail or market value) as part of inventory. See Inventory.
   Expense category: For gifts, Office Expenses.
   More information: IRS Publication 463, *Travel, Gift, and Car Expenses.*
   Employers: Cash gifts to employees, "cash equivalents" such as gift cards and gift certificates, and items of significant value are considered taxable wages, subject to payroll taxes. Small nonmonetary gifts, such as a Thanksgiving turkey or a birthday gift, are deductible and are not considered part of the employee's wages. Gifts to employees are not subject to the $25 cost limit.

Business Income Deduction

Some businesses can deduct 20% of the net profit in figuring their income taxes. See Qualified Business Income Deduction. This deduction expires after 2025.

Business Licenses

Business licenses, registrations, and similar fees are deductible.
Expense category: Taxes and Licenses.

Business Opportunity

Business opportunity refers to a packaged business system, sort of a start-your-own-business kit or plan that you can buy to start your own small business, such as a cleaning system, a vending machine route, a sales cart, or a distributorship arrangement, that might include training guides and possibly inventory and equipment.

Deductions for business opportunities depend on what you are actually buying: an idea or instructions, equipment, inventory, supplies. Deductions also depend on whether you are already in business when you make the purchases.

If this is a brand new business you are starting, deductions for startup costs are limited. See Buying a Business and Startup Costs. If you are starting a corporation, also see Organizational Costs.

If you are already in business and are expanding or branching out, each component of the purchase is deducted separately, which might be tricky to allocate and prorate. I suggest getting help from an experienced accountant.
Expense category: Depends on what you are purchasing.

Business Trips

Business trips are deductible, but there are many rules and restrictions. See Travel.

Business Use of Your Home

See Home Expenses.

Count the day won when the earth, turning on its axis, imposes no additional taxes.

—F. P. Adams, *New York Evening Mail*, 1834

Buying a Business

There are four ways someone might buy a business:

1. Purchasing a business from the former owner of the business.
2. Buying a franchise where you become a franchisee, purchasing the right to the franchise name and operating as though your business was part of a much larger operation.
3. Buying into a direct-sales (multilevel, networking) program, usually where you buy and resell consumer goods, often cosmetics, vitamins, or kitchenware.
4. Buying a business opportunity package or kit as described above under Business Opportunity.

Each type of business has different rules:

Buying an independent business: When you buy someone else's business, some of the purchase price is deductible, some of the cost is depreciated over several years, and some of the cost may not be deductible at all. A lot depends on how the business is structured legally (corporation, partnership, LLC, or sole proprietorship) and what the purchase agreement says. The precise legal wording can affect how the sale is taxed, how the assets are valued for tax purposes, and how much of the purchase price will be deductible.

For most business purchases, you are not actually buying a business, you are buying a collection of assets that are part of a business: equipment, furniture and fixtures, inventory, supplies, possibly a building, possibly the accounts receivable, possibly the debts and liabilities. The purchase price sometimes includes a covenant not to compete: the seller agrees not to start another business that will be in competition with the one you are buying.

You may also be buying what's called goodwill, money you are paying above the actual value of the assets. An ongoing successful business is worth more than a new untested business. That "worth more" is the goodwill, obviously a very subjective value, and the reason goodwill is also called "blue sky" (as in "picking a number out of thin air").

Each component of the business (assets, inventory, goodwill, commissions) is valued separately, and each component comes under different tax deduction rules. You may also be paying a business broker's commission. A lot of tax money is at stake here. You should talk to an experienced tax accountant before signing any agreement.

Expense category: Depends on what is being purchased.

Buying a franchise, business opportunity, or direct-sales distributorship: Tax deductions for buying a franchise or other prepackaged business opportunity depend on what you are actually purchasing. A one-time fee to become a franchisee or distributor is considered an intangible asset and is amortized over fifteen years. Ongoing annual franchise or distributor fees can be written off when paid (*Expense category:* Other Expenses). Costs for equipment, inventory and supplies are deducted under the rules for the specific items you are purchasing. Also see Startup Costs and, for corporations, Organizational Costs.

Cafeteria

Employers can deduct 50% of the cost of operating a company cafeteria if more than half of the meals eaten there were served to employees who needed to be available during their meal breaks, or because there were no other reasonable meal alternatives for the employees.

Expense category: Varies depending on actual expenses.

Cafeteria Plan

This is a term for an employee fringe benefit plan, also known as a Flexible Spending Account, where you can reimburse employee medical and child care expenses. Employees get to choose from several fringe benefit options, sort of like choosing food from a cafeteria.

If set up properly, the costs of a cafeteria plan are deductible for you, the employer, and not taxable to your employees. This will require the help of an experienced accountant.

Expense category: Employee Benefit Programs.

More information: IRS Publication 15-B, *Employer's Guide to Fringe Benefits*.

Corporations: Owner-employees of regular C corporations are eligible for most employee fringe benefits, but owner-employees of S corporations are usually not eligible. Check each listing to see which types of businesses qualify.

Campaign Contributions

Political contributions are not deductible.

Cancellation Penalties

Cancellation penalties are deductible.
   Expense category: Other Expenses.

Capitalized Expenses

Capitalize is a tax term that means the cost of an asset is deducted over a period of years instead of being deducted the year incurred. For tangible assets, the deduction is called depreciation. For intangible assets such as patents and trademarks, the deduction is called amortization. Look up individual assets to see which assets can, or must, be capitalized.

Carrying Charges

A carrying charge is a service charge or financing charge for buying something on time, in installments, or on layaway. Carrying charges are treated like interest charges and are usually deductible. See Interest.
   Expense category: Interest.

Cars

You can deduct the cost of using a car for business or you can take the Standard Mileage Rate, but with limitations. See Vehicles.

Cartons

Cartons, boxes, and other containers and packaging used to hold the goods you sell are considered part of your inventory.

If, however, the cost of containers or packaging is not significant, or containers are used only occasionally, most businesses write them off currently as shipping supplies or office supplies.

Expense category: Supplies.

Carts

Vending carts and other carts used for business can be deducted the year purchased and first used in the business, or at your option, depreciated over seven years. For details and special situations, see Business Assets.

Expense category: Depreciation or Other Expenses, depending on several factors. See Business Assets.

Millions of small businesses contribute daily to the economic success of our nation. They pay taxes.

—Former Senator Robert Dole

Casualty and Theft Losses

Business losses from fire, storm, or other casualty or from theft or vandalism may or may not be deductible as a business expense.

Losses that are covered by insurance are not deductible.

You cannot take a deduction for damaged or stolen assets that have already been deducted. Machinery and equipment, furniture, inventory, supplies, or other assets deducted when purchased cannot be deducted a second time as a loss.

Uninsured business assets that are being depreciated and not already fully written off (most buildings) can be depreciated further, up to the undepreciated balance.

Inventory that is stolen or damaged that has not already been deducted (if you are using the accrual method of accounting) can be written off as cost of goods sold. See Inventory.

Cleaning and repairing damage is deductible.

Any other business losses, including stolen cash, are deductible—but not as a business deduction. The deduction is taken on your 1040 tax return, and then only if you itemize deductions. This is a raw deal for businesses that were robbed, not being able to deduct the stolen cash as a business deduction, but that's the law.

Insured property: Any loss covered by insurance is not deductible. If you have insurance, you are required to file a claim with the insurance company or you cannot take a tax deduction on any of the insured property. If the insurance policy has a deductible (a portion of the loss you pay), the amount you pay is tax deductible, under the above rules.

Proof of loss: The IRS requires proof of casualty losses. Take photos, make a list of everything affected, and if theft or vandalism is involved, file a police report. Theft and vandalism losses are deducted the year discovered regardless of the year they occurred.

Expense category: Depends on what is being deducted.

More information: IRS Publication 547, *Casualties, Disasters, and Thefts*.

Cell Phones/Smartphones

Cell phones (cellular phones) and smartphones can be deducted the year purchased and first used in the business, or at your option, depreciated over seven years. For details and special situations, see Business Assets.

You can also deduct the cost of any contract and the monthly fees.

Expense category: For contracts and fees, Office Expenses. For purchase, Depreciation or Other Expenses, depending on several factors. See Business Assets.

Part business, part personal: If your phone is used partly for business, you can deduct the percentage of the cost used for business. Determining the percentage used for business (incoming and outgoing calls and text messages and whatever else you are using the phone for) can be a real nuisance, and most businesses estimate usage. If you are audited, however, and you don't have a record of your business usage, an IRS auditor could disallow the deduction, but probably wouldn't. I suggest keeping a record if you can, and making an honest estimate if you can't. An auditor would have to be in a mighty bad mood to disallow the deduction.

CGS

"CGS" stands for cost of goods sold. See Inventory.

Chargebacks

All business-related chargebacks are deductible.

Expense category: Depends on what the chargeback is for. If you aren't sure, use Office Expenses.

Charitable Contributions

See Donations.

Chauffeur

As I mentioned in chapter 3, all business expenses, in order to be deductible, must meet three IRS requirements. They must be (1) ordinary, (2) necessary, and (3) not lavish or extravagant. If you can look an underpaid, underappreciated IRS agent in the eye and convince him that the cost of hiring your personal chauffeur is ordinary, necessary, and not lavish or extravagant, I congratulate you.

Seriously, though, there could be a business situation (for example, when you want to make an impression on a client) where a chauffeur is appropriate, and deductible. Be aware that you may be walking a fine line between promoting your business, which is fully deductible, and entertainment, which is not deductible. You may want to discuss this deduction with a tax accountant.

Expense category: Legal and Professional Services.

IRS Red Flag Audit Warning: If this deduction is not going to save you a lot of tax money, I suggest that you consider not taking it.

Child Care

See Dependent Care.

Child care business: Expenses for running a child care business are deductible like the expenses of any other business, including meals served to the children (with exceptions; see Meals). If you run a child care business out of your home, see Home Expenses for the child care deductions allowed.

Children on Payroll

You can hire your children and get a business tax deduction for their wages. And within certain limitations, there is no income tax and no payroll taxes on the children's wages.

This deduction for your children applies to sole proprietorships, spousal partnerships, spousal joint ventures, and one-person LLCs. It does not apply to corporations, regular partnerships, or multi-owner LLCs.

The rules are very specific, but generally, if you have children under eighteen years old, you can pay each of your children who qualify up to $13,850 a year tax free and get a business deduction for the wages. The maximum amount changes from year to year; it is the same as the standard deduction for unmarried individuals.

The children should be doing legitimate, business-related work to justify the salary earned. You can't hire your seventeen-year-old to babysit your three-year-old and get the deduction.

The children do not have to file a federal income tax return, and they owe no federal income taxes. And you, the parent-employer, get a full tax deduction for the wages paid. It's a rare tax law indeed that lets you have your cake and eat it too.

If your child has what's called unearned income, such as bank interest, that income cannot exceed $2,500, and the child's total income, wages and all other taxable sources, cannot exceed $13,850.

If the child does have excess unearned income, or if the child is earning more than the $13,850 income maximum, he or she is required to file an income tax return. But the child's wages, regardless of the amount paid, are exempt from Social Security and Medicare taxes.

You will need to fill out a W-4 payroll form for each child (but it does not need to be sent to the IRS) and, at year end, file W-2 and W-3 payroll forms as you would for any employee, but no payroll taxes are due. You do not need to file a 941 or 944 payroll tax return.

Expense category: Wages.

More Information: IRS Publication 15, *Employer's Tax Guide.*

State taxes: Check with your state employment department before you hire your children. Many states have similar laws to the IRS, impose no state income or payroll taxes, nor require workers' compensation insurance on your children. Check your state employer's guide. Do not rely on verbal information. People who work at state employment departments are often unaware of child employment laws.

Children who hire their parents: The parents are considered regular employees, subject to all regular income and employment taxes except Federal Unemployment Tax (FUTA).

There's nothing wrong with the younger generation that becoming a taxpayer won't cure.

—Columnist Dan Bennett

Classes

Many classes and education expenses are deductible. See Education.

Cleaning Service

Cleaning and janitorial services for the business premises are deductible. Cleaning and laundry services for clothing used exclusively for work are deductible if the clothing is unsuitable for street wear, such as a uniform, costume, or protective gear. Clothing with your company's logo or advertising is also deductible. See Clothing.

Cleaning and laundry services for your regular clothing are deductible when you are traveling away from home overnight on business.

Expense category: Office Expenses. If traveling, Travel.

Home-Based Business: Cleaning services for the business portion of the home are part of the Home Expenses deduction, not deducted separately. See Home Expenses.

There is universal reluctance to voluntarily pay taxes.

—Society of California Accountants

Closing Costs

Loan closing costs include broker commission, processing fees, title insurance, property taxes, termite reports, transfer taxes, loan fees, points, and other costs. Some of these closing costs are deductible immediately; some are deducted over a period of years. This is a complicated area of law that may need the help of an experienced accountant.

Expense category: Varies depending on actual expenses.

Clothing

Clothing used exclusively for work and unsuitable for street wear is deductible.

The term "unsuitable for street wear" was written into law more than fifty years ago. Today, it's hard to say what is considered unsuitable for street wear. Clothing with your company logo or advertising is deductible,

Tax deduction for the whole family. The late New Orleans R&B legend Oliver "La La" Morgan had one hit record, "Who Shot the La La"; he never tired of promoting it, or himself.

even though the clothing is suitable for street wear. Uniforms, costumes, and protective gear are deductible. Cost of cleaning is deductible.

Expense category: Supplies.

Musicians and entertainers: Stage outfits and tuxedos are deductible. Stage costume jewelry is deductible. Clothing with your stage name or your band name or logo is deductible.

Cloud Computing

Cost of renting, leasing, or subscribing to cloud software and storage is deductible.

Expense category: Office Expenses.

Clubs

Most club dues are not deductible, including business clubs. Dues to service clubs such as Rotary and Lions are deductible. Dues to merchant associations and professional organizations are deductible. See Associations.

Expense category: If deductible, Other Expenses.

Club owners: This deduction does not apply to clubs you own.

Coffee Service

Deductible. Deductible. Deductible. Thank you.

Expense category: Office Expenses.

If you want to know how anyone can stop paying taxes, the answer seems to be: the same way porcupines make love. Very, very gingerly.

—Samuel Thesham, accountant of the Wild West

Collection Agency

Fees charged by collection agencies are deductible.

For businesses on the cash method of accounting (most small businesses), accounts turned over to collection agencies should be added to income at the time the money comes in: the amount you actually receive, not the full amount owed you.

Accounts that collection agencies are unable to collect cannot be deducted as a bad debt. You cannot deduct income that you earned but never received.

Expense category: Legal and Professional Services.

Commissions

Commissions that you pay to outside salespeople or companies and commissions paid for referrals, finders fees, and the like are deductible. However, see Sales Reps for very important information on how to deduct what you pay them.

Commissions that you pay to acquire new customers who sign long-term contracts may have to be amortized over a period of years. The IRS says the deduction should be spread over the average number of years new customers stay with the business.

Real estate commissions are added to the cost of the real estate and depreciated. See Depreciation.

A business broker's commission for helping to buy or sell a business may have to be amortized over five years. See Buying a Business.

Expense category: If deductible, Commissions and Fees. If amortized, Other Expenses.

Community Donations

Community service expenses and donations to community organizations that bring recognition or publicity to your business may be deductible, depending on what is being donated. See Donations.

We hang the petty thieves, but appoint the great ones to public office.

—Aesop, 600 B.C.

Commuting

Commuting expenses, home to your regular place of business and back, are not deductible.

IRS Red Flag Audit Alert: For some reason, the IRS really goes after small businesses that deduct the cost of going to work: a lousy 58-cents-a-mile deduction that you can't take.

Home-Based Business: Home business owners do not commute to work, but there is one fine point in the commute law. If you drive to clients or customers, the IRS considers the trip from your home to your first client a commute, not deductible. The same goes for the trip home from your last call of the day. The IRS says the trip home is a commute. There may be a way to avoid this loss of a deduction. If you go to your home office and do some work before you visit your first client, most accountants feel that you already did your commute (to your office), and that your first client visit is deductible. Ditto for returning home after visiting your last client, if you return to your office to work before quitting for the day. Pretty picky rules here, I admit. Part of the secret to success in business is (1) knowing the rules and (2) knowing how to break them.

Compensation

Self-employed people cannot take a deduction for compensation you pay to yourself. See Paying Yourself. Compensation paid to any independent contractor or other person who is not an employee is deductible. See Independent Contractors.

Employers: Compensation to employees is deductible. See Wages.

Corporations: Owners of corporations are employees of their businesses. Your compensation is treated like any other employee wages. See Wages.

Computer Programs

See Software.

Computers

Computers and peripherals (monitors, printers) can be deducted the year purchased and first used in the business, or at your option, depreciated over five years. For details and special situations, see Business Assets.

Expense category: Depreciation or Other Expenses, depending on several factors. See Business Assets.

Part business, part personal: If your computer is used partly for nonbusiness purposes, you can deduct the percentage of the cost used for business.

Condominium

Business condominiums that you rent or lease are deductible.

Expense category: Rent or Lease.

Business condominiums that you own are depreciated like any other business building. See Depreciation.

Expense category: Depreciation.

More information: IRS Publication 946, *How to Depreciate Property.*

Condominium associations, management fees, and other charges are deductible if business related.

Expense category: Legal and Professional Services.

IRS Red Flag Audit Warning: Deducting a condo is one mighty fast way to invite an audit. I highly suggest that you discuss this with an experienced accountant.

Home-Based Business: Buildings are part of the Home Expenses deduction, not deducted separately. See Home Expenses.

The Higher the Tax Bracket, the Better the View.

—Advertisement for a luxury Florida real estate development

Conferences

Costs of conducting or attending business conferences are deductible. Travel is deductible. Meals are 50% deductible. See Travel.

Expense category: Other Expenses (for the conference itself).

IRS Red Flag Audit Warning: Travel is always a deduction that catches IRS attention. See Travel for suggestions on how to avoid—and, if necessary, how to prepare for—audits.

Consignment

The deduction for consigned merchandise is different for the consignor (the business that owns the merchandise) and the consignee (the business that sells the merchandise).

Consignor: Merchandise that you own and consign to another business is inventory. If the inventory was deducted when you purchased the merchandise or the materials to manufacture the merchandise, there is no additional deduction. If you use cost-of-goods-sold accrual accounting, you deduct your cost when the consignee sells the merchandise and pays you. If you don't know the difference between the two options, see Inventory.

Consignee: Merchandise that you take on consignment is not deducted until you sell the merchandise and pay the consignee. What you pay is deducted as an inventory expense.

How consignment works: Consignment refers to merchandise that a business or self-employed individual places with another business for the other business to sell. For example, a dressmaker may consign inventory to a dress shop. The business consigning the goods (the consignor, the dressmaker) has not made a sale and does not get paid until the business that has taken the goods on consignment (the consignee, the dress shop) sells the goods.

The dress shop deducts the cost of the merchandise (the amount the shop pays the dressmaker) when the shop pays the dressmaker. The dressmaker deducts the cost of the merchandise either when the merchandise is purchased or when sold, depending on how the dressmaker deducts inventory, as explained under Inventory.

The dressmaker does not get a deduction for time devoted to making the dress. Your own time is not a deductible expense (unless you are incorporated). See Paying Yourself.

Expense category: Inventory.

Bankruptcy and consignment: Consignors should be warned that these consignment laws are income tax laws only. They may not hold up in bankruptcy court. If the dress shop files for bankruptcy before it sells the dress, the court can seize and sell consigned inventory to pay off the creditors of the dress shop, even though the shop doesn't legally own the goods. The dressmaker will have to stand in line with all the other creditors hoping to get paid.

The dressmaker can protect herself/himself by filing what's known as a UCC-1 form with the county or state where the dress shop is located (UCC stands for Uniform Commercial Code). This is a legal notice that the goods belong to the dressmaker and not to the dress shop. It will usually hold up in bankruptcy court, enabling the consignor to get the unsold merchandise back. If the dress was sold by the dress shop but the shop filed for bankruptcy before paying the dressmaker, the dressmaker is just another creditor who probably will never see any money. A UCC-1 filing will not help.

If you are the consignor (the dressmaker in our example), if the consignee (the dress shop) is bankrupt and you cannot get paid or get the dress back, you cannot take a tax deduction for the loss (explained under Casualty Losses) and, sadly, there also is no deduction for the lost income. The message here is that consignors need to keep an eye on their products, and on the businesses entrusted with the products.

Construction

How construction costs are deducted depends on what is being constructed. For buildings, see Buildings. For built-in additions or renovations to buildings, see Building Improvements. For machinery or equipment, see Business Assets. If you are constructing or manufacturing merchandise to sell, see Inventory.

Home-Based Business: Buildings and built-in components are part of the Home Expenses deduction, not deducted separately. See Home Expenses.

Construction Equipment

Heavy construction equipment like tractors, excavators, and dump trucks can be deducted the year purchased and first used in the business, or at your option, depreciated over several years (five years for vehicles, seven years for machinery). For details and special situations, see Business Assets.

Expense category: Depreciation or Other Expenses, depending on several factors. See Business Assets.

Some tax cutting strategies make good financial sense. Other tax strategies are simply bad ideas, often because tax considerations are allowed to override basic economics.

—CPA Jim Angell, Willits, California

Consultants

Definition of a consultant: Someone who saves his client almost enough money to pay his fee. Consultant fees are deductible.
Expense category: Commissions and Fees.

Containers

Boxes, cartons, and other containers and packaging materials that hold the goods you sell are considered part of your inventory. See Inventory. If, however, the cost of the containers or packaging is not significant or the containers are used only occasionally, most businesses deduct them as a current expense.
Expense category: Supplies.

Contamination Cleanup

If the cost is minor, the cleanup can be deducted. The IRS considers any expense of $2,500 or less to be minor.
   If the cost is significant, it may have to be added to the cost of the land, which means no deduction until you sell the land. If you have significant contamination costs, I suggest you talk to an experienced accountant.
   The cost of contamination cleanup from manufacturing is added to the cost of the inventory. See Inventory.
Expense category: If minor, Other Expenses. If inventory, Inventory.

Contests

The cost of holding a contest that generates publicity or sales for your business is deductible. The prizes given out are deductible, but prizes have tax problems you should know about. See Prizes.

Expense category: For the cost of holding a contest, Advertising. If the prize is merchandise you normally sell, Inventory. If the prize is something other than your merchandise, Advertising.

Contract Labor

The term *contract labor* refers to independent contractors. See Independent Contractors. Also see Temporary Help Agency.

Contractors (Building)

Minor work and repairs can be deducted currently. See Repairs.

Building contractor fees for new construction are added to the cost of the building and depreciated. Contractor fees for doing major renovations may have to be added to the cost of the building or may be deducted currently, depending on the situation. See Depreciation, and see Building Improvements.

Expense category: If minor, Repairs. If new construction or renovations, Depreciation.

Independent contractors: Independent contractors are self-employed people, who could be doing any kind of work. Independent contractors come under a different set of laws than building contractors. See Independent Contractors.

Home-Based Business: Building costs and repairs are part of the Home Expenses deduction, not deducted separately. See Home Expenses.

Contracts

The cost of preparing a contract is deductible if it is not a substantial amount of money. Contracts that are expensive to negotiate and prepare and cover more than a year are amortized over the length of the contract. A payment to be released from a contract is deductible.

Expense category: If deductible currently, Legal and Professional Services. If amortized, Other Expenses. If contract release, Other Expenses.

Service contracts and extended warranties can be deducted currently if they do not exceed twelve months. If they do exceed twelve months, see Prepayments.

Expense category: Office Expenses.

Love the heavenly creator, but fill the earthly treasure
If rulers must gather tolls, taxes and tribute
Let no one refuse the debt that he owes.

—Johann Sebastian Bach, *Nur jedem das Seine*, 1715

Contributions

Money you contribute to your own business is neither income nor expense, and it is not deductible. Political contributions are not deductible. Charitable and community contributions are sometimes deductible; see Donations.

Conventions

The cost of attending a business convention is deductible. Travel and lodging expenses are deductible. Meals are 50% deductible.

The expense of a spouse traveling with you is not deductible unless the spouse is a partner or employee in the business and has a valid business reason for attending. See Travel.

Expense category: Travel.

More information: IRS Publication 463, *Travel, Gift, and Car Expenses.*

IRS Red Flag Audit Warning: Travel is always a deduction that catches IRS attention. See Travel for suggestions on how to avoid—and, if necessary, how to prepare for—audits.

Copies

Deductible.

Expense category: Office Supplies.

Copyrights

The IRS says that a copyright is amortized over fifteen years.

Last time I checked with the U.S. Copyright Office, it costs $35 to obtain a copyright. So following the IRS regulations, you can deduct $2.30 a year for fifteen years. Me, I'd deduct the $35 the year I pay it and hope the statute of limitations runs out before they catch me.

Expense category: If obeying the law, Amortization. If disobeying the law, which of course I do not recommend, Taxes and Licenses.

Cost of Goods Sold (CGS)

Cost of goods sold is a method of deducting inventory used by businesses that use accrual accounting, deducting the cost of the inventory when sold, not when purchased. If you are unsure which method to use, cash or accrual, read the pros and cons under Inventory. And if you don't know what I'm talking about, read "Cash Method versus Accrual Accounting" in chapter 1.

If you will be using the cash accounting method, deducting your inventory when you purchase it, you can skip this entire entry. If you decided to use the accrual accounting method, the calculations and all of the rules are explained below.

Calculating cost of goods sold is a three-step procedure:

Step One: Start with the cost of your inventory on hand at the beginning of the year. If you had no inventory, you start with $0.

Step Two: Add all the inventory purchases during the year. Beginning inventory (from Step One) plus your purchases during the year gives you the total inventory available for sale during the year.

Step Three: Subtract the ending inventory: the cost of inventory still on hand at the end of the year. The resulting figure is your cost of goods sold: inventory at January 1, plus purchases during the year, minus inventory on hand December 31, equals cost of goods sold.

To accomplish Step Three, make a list of inventory on hand at the end of the year. This is called taking inventory or taking a physical inventory. The word *inventory* refers to both the goods and to the procedure of counting the goods. Inventory on hand at year end is usually valued at its cost to you and not at its sales price.

If for any reason your year-end inventory is worth less than what you paid, the inventory should be valued at this lesser amount. "Worth" refers to its retail value, what you can sell it for. If year-end inventory is totally worthless, it should be valued at zero. This inventory valuation method is known as lower of cost or market: You value your year-end inventory at its cost or at its market value, whichever is less. Lowering the value ("writing down") damaged or unsalable merchandise increases your cost of goods sold, thereby decreasing your profits, and decreasing your taxes.

If you do value your inventory at less than its cost, the IRS requires you to offer the devalued inventory for sale at the lower-than-market price, either before year end or within thirty days after the year end. You don't have to actually sell the inventory, but you do need to offer it for sale. If you have worthless inventory (valued at zero dollars), the IRS has stated that you must dispose of the inventory to get the deduction.

Inventory missing, stolen, or given away: The cost of stolen or missing inventory and the cost of samples given away are deductible as part of cost of goods sold. This missing inventory is not on hand at year end, so it is not included in your year-end inventory count. It automatically becomes part of your cost of goods sold, even though it really wasn't sold. The term *cost of goods sold* really should be *cost of goods sold, lost, stolen, given away, damaged, or unsalable.*

Manufacturers and crafts businesses: The cost of inventory on hand at the end of the year includes not just your materials and manufacturing supplies (inventory you have not yet worked on) but also any finished and partially finished goods. Value your finished and partly finished inventory at its cost to you. That cost includes materials and paid labor. It does not include your own labor, unless you are an employee of your own corporation.

Consignment: Consigned inventory is merchandise one business or self-employed individual places with another business for the other business to try to sell. Consigned inventory belongs to the consignor (the business that produced the inventory), not the consignee (the business trying to sell the inventory). The inventory, if unsold at year end, is part of the consignor's ending inventory. See Consignment.

Expense category: Cost of Goods Sold.

Costumes

Clothing used exclusively for work and unsuitable for street wear is deductible. Cost of cleaning is deductible. See Clothing.

Expense category: Supplies.

Courier Service

Any business service of this type is deductible.
Expense category: Office Expenses.

Covenant Not to Compete

A covenant not to compete is a contract where the seller of a business agrees not to start another business that will be in competition with the one you are buying. Often included as part of the purchase price of a business, a covenant not to compete can be amortized over fifteen years. See Buying a Business.
Expense category: Other Expenses.

Give me a list of write-offs organized by type of deduction, and you're guaranteed to knock half off your tax preparation bill.

—CPA Andrew Blackman, New York City

Credentials

The cost of education to obtain a credential is deductible in some situations, but not others. See Education.

Credit Cards and Debit Cards

Business purchases made with a credit card or debit card are fully deductible. You can use your personal credit or debit card for business purchases and get a full business deduction for business purchases (sole proprietors and one-person LLC owners only).

Credit and debit card fees and interest are also deductible. If the card is used partly for business, you prorate any bank charges, fees and interest, personal versus business.

Expense category: For purchases, the category depends on what was purchased. For bank fees, Office Expenses. For interest charges, Interest.

Corporations, partnerships, and multi-owner LLCs: To maximize tax deductions and minimize paperwork, corporations, partnerships, and multi-owner LLCs should have credit and debit cards in the business name, not in the owner's or employee's name. If you do use your personal card to pay business bills, to get the best tax advantage, have the business reimburse you for your expenses. See Reimbursements.

Credits

If you receive a credit reducing the cost of goods or services you are buying, treat the credit like a discounted price. Do not list the credit as a separate item in your records or on your tax return.

If a credit is a refund for something you previously bought, reduce or delete the expense previously recorded. If the expense was from a prior year, add the refund to your income for the current year.

Expense category: If reducing expenses, whatever category was used for the original expense.

Also see Tax Credits.

Cryptocurrency

Business expenses paid in bitcoins and other cryptocurrencies (digital or virtual currencies) are deductible as barter transactions. The amount of the expense is the fair market value of the goods or services you are getting in exchange for the bitcoins. See Barter/Trade.

Also be aware that the IRS treats cryptocurrency as property. If you are using appreciated bitcoin or similar currencies to pay expenses or to pay taxes, you will have a taxable gain to the extent of appreciation from the date you acquired it and the date you spend it.

Expense category: Depends on the type of expense.

IRS Red Flag Audit Warning: The U.S. Department of Justice thinks that anyone using bitcoins is likely to be involved in illegal activities or tax fraud, and it has instructed IRS agents to be looking for bitcoin activity.

Customer List

A customer list that you purchase is considered an intangible asset, which usually has to be amortized over fifteen years. However, if it isn't a significant amount ($2,500 or less), most businesses just deduct it currently.

Expense category: If deducting, Office Expenses. If amortizing, Other Expenses.

Customs

Customs duties and all fees and taxes related to importing and exporting can be deducted, although these expenses can sometimes be added to the cost of the inventory being purchased or sold. You may want to talk to an accountant with export and import experience.

Expense category: For duties and tariffs, Taxes and Licenses. For non-government fees, Legal and Professional Services. If adding to the cost of the inventory, Inventory.

Damaged Property

If business assets are damaged or destroyed, you are entitled to a deduction. See Casualty Losses. If inventory is damaged or destroyed, it can be deducted as inventory. See Inventory.

Damages

Penalties for breach of contract are sometimes called damages. They are deductible.

Expense category: Other Expenses.

Damage to business property may be deductible. See Casualty Losses.

Damaged inventory is deductible. See Inventory.

Legal damages (court-awarded payments) are usually deductible. See Lawsuits.

Database

A database that you purchase is considered an intangible asset, which usually must be amortized over fifteen years. However, if it isn't a significant amount ($2,500 or less), most businesses just deduct it currently.

Expense category: If deducting, Office Expenses. If amortizing, Other Expenses.

Day Care

See Dependent Care.

Day care business: Expenses for running a day care business are deductible like the expenses of any other business, including meals served (with exceptions; see Meals). If you run a day care business out of your home, see Home Expenses for the day care deductions allowed.

Debit Cards

Debit card fees and expenses are handled the same as credit cards. See Credit Cards.

Decorating

Decorating expenses are deductible.

Expense category: Office Expenses.

Valuable art treasures and antiques come under different rules. See Antiques.

Home-Based Business: Office decorating costs are part of the Home Expenses deduction, not deducted separately. See Home Expenses.

Why does a slight tax increase cost you $200, and a substantial tax cut save you 30 cents?

—Business owner Peg Bracken

Delivery Charges

Delivery charges for goods you sell are deductible. Weekly delivery service charges on a contract with UPS, FedEx, or other delivery service are deductible.

Delivery charges for inventory you are buying are added to the cost of the inventory. See Inventory. Delivery charges for business assets you are buying (machinery, equipment, furniture) should be added to the cost of the asset. See Business Assets.

Expense category: For delivery charges on merchandise you sell, Other Expenses. For weekly service charges, Office Expenses.

De Minimis Safe Harbor

This is a method for deducting the cost of business assets and building improvements and renovations. See Safe Harbor.

Demolition

The cost to demolish a building is added to the cost basis of the land. It cannot be deducted or depreciated.

Cost of removing storage tanks is deductible.

Expense category: Other Expenses.

Demonstration Costs and Products

Costs incurred to demonstrate a product or service you are selling are deductible. The cost of the products are deductible as inventory.

Expense category: Cost of demonstrations, Advertising. Cost of the products themselves, Inventory.

Government isn't religion. It shouldn't be treated as such. It's not God. It's humans, fallible people, feathering their nests most of the time.

—Former California Governor Jerry Brown

Dependent Care

You can deduct up to $5,000 a year for child and dependent care for your own children or dependents. The deduction cannot exceed your net profit from the business.

If you are married, both spouses must have jobs or be looking for jobs, or one spouse must be a full-time student or unable to care for him- or herself. There are additional rules and limitations for married people and on how the money can be spent.

Employers: Dependent care provided for your employees' families is deductible. You can also pay employees money for them to spend on dependent care, tax free to the employees, up to $5,000 per year. You, the employer, get a deduction. You can take the deduction for your own family only if you offer the same assistance to your employees. If you provide child care facilities for your employees, you may be eligible for an Employer's Child Care Tax Credit. See Tax Credits.

More information: IRS Publication 503, *Child and Dependent Care Expenses.*

Child care business: Expenses for running a child care business are deductible like the expenses of any other business, including meals served to the children; see Meals. If you run a child care business out of your home, see Home Expenses for the child care deductions allowed.

Depletion

If you own mineral property or standing timber, you can take a deduction for depletion. This is a complex area of tax law that will require help from an experienced accountant.

Expense category: Depletion.

Deposits

Nonrefundable deposits are deductible when you make the deposit.

Refundable deposits are not deductible. This applies to rent and cleaning deposits, deposits required by utility companies, sales tax deposits, or any other deposits where you will get your money back. If you do not get your money back, if whoever has the deposit applies it to the rent or whatever it was for, you can deduct the amount of the deposit at that time.

Expense category: Depends on what you are purchasing.

Advances and down payments: The terms *advances*, *deposits*, and *down payments* are often used interchangeably. An advance or down payment is really a prepayment for work to be done or goods to be delivered, not money you expect to get back. Advances are deductible. See Advances.

Bank deposits are not deductible. They are not expenses. But you know that.

The Revenue Act of 1791 was the first tax law passed by the U.S. Congress. It was a tax on whiskey and tobacco.

Depreciable Assets

Depreciable assets are business assets that are eligible for depreciation, although most depreciable assets can be deducted the year of purchase instead of being depreciated. See Business Assets.

Depreciation

Most tangible assets other than buildings can either be depreciated, or at your option, deducted when purchased. Most buildings must be depreciated. Different assets have different depreciation rules and write-off periods (number of years).

Depreciation is a tax term and means that the tax deduction for the cost of a business asset—buildings, vehicles, machinery, equipment, furniture— is spread out over several years. When you depreciate an asset, you do not deduct the entire cost of the asset the year you purchase it. Each year, a portion of the cost is deducted.

Intangible assets such as trademarks and patents are not depreciated. They are amortized, which basically means the same thing. Look up individual intangible assets for their specific tax details.

Deducting instead of depreciating: Depreciation is a complicated deduction that most businesses avoid by deducting assets (other than most buildings) the year of purchase instead of depreciating them. While this simplifies taxes, it may or may not be to your advantage.

Many new businesses make little or no profit the first year or two, and may owe little or no income tax. Rather than take a full deduction for business assets when you purchase them, it might be better to depreciate the assets, spreading the deduction over several years. In this way, you deduct the bulk of the expense in future years when you can use it to save taxes.

You can depreciate some assets and write off others. It is not all one way or the other. You might want to calculate (or hire an accountant to calculate) your profit and taxes under both methods to find the bigger tax savings.

But if you want to deduct the full cost of your business assets instead of depreciating them, the rules are explained under Business Assets. No need to read any more of this entry.

Depreciating assets: What can be depreciated? Depreciable assets include buildings, components of buildings, vehicles, machinery, shop equipment, office equipment, furniture, fixtures, tools, aircraft, boats, trailers, some farm animals, plants, and trees. Major building improvements and major repairs that extend the life of an asset can be depreciated. Both new and used assets can be depreciated. Depreciable assets are also called fixed assets or, as they are throughout this book, business assets.

What cannot be depreciated? Inventory, supplies, inexpensive tools, or anything that will not last more than a year cannot be depreciated. Land cannot be depreciated or written off until sold, but some land improvements, including parking lots and landscaping, can be depreciated.

Different assets have different numbers of years they can be depreciated, called write-off periods or recovery periods or useful life:

3 years: Software you purchase or develop, on-road tractor units, racehorses over two years old, all horses over twelve years old.

5 years: Vehicles, trailers, aircraft, computers, office equipment, carpeting, movable partitions, outdoor lighting, equipment used for research and experimentation, farm equipment, semiconductor manufacturing equipment, some alternative energy property such as solar and wind, some electronic equipment, some software you develop, movable gasoline storage tanks, appliances and furniture used in residential rental property.

7 years: Most machinery other than farm equipment, furniture, fixtures, most signs, vending machines, railroad track, horses other than those listed under "3 years."

10 years: Most boats, single-purpose agricultural and horticultural structures, fruit and nut trees, vines.

15 years: Large outdoor signs, gas stations including their minimarts, many building renovations, leasehold improvements, parking lots, major landscaping.

20 years: All-purpose farm buildings.

27½ years: Residential rental buildings. For business use of your home, if your home is part of an apartment building that you own.

39 years: All buildings other than those listed above. For business use of your home, if your home is a single-family residence.

Other: Assets that were purchased before going into business can be depreciated regardless of when acquired. These assets are valued at their cost or at their market value at the time the assets are first used in your business, whichever is less. If some old machinery that cost you $2,000 eight years ago was worth only $500 (market value) when first used in your business, you may depreciate only $500.

Depreciation methods: There are four methods of depreciation, each requiring different calculations. All four methods result in the same tax write-off eventually, but each method involves different amounts that can be deducted in any given year. For some assets, you can choose which depreciation method you want to use. Other assets must use a specific method. There are additional rules for the first year an asset is depreciated, and additional calculations if you sell or abandon an asset. The methods and rules are explained in detail in the IRS publication mentioned below, if you want to study and compare them. There is no way to simplify the procedure, other than using tax software or hiring an accountant.

Part business, part nonbusiness: Assets used partly for business and partly for nonbusiness can be depreciated to the extent used for business. For example, if you use your tools 50% for business and 50% for personal use, you can depreciate 50% of the cost.

Bonus depreciation: Most tangible assets with a write-off period of twenty years or less are eligible for bonus depreciation (through 2026), which allows you to deduct a percentage of the cost of assets when you purchase them. Bonus depreciation is optional. The amount you can deduct drops every year through 2026, after which the deduction is eliminated. See Business Assets for more information.

Expense category: Depreciation.

More information: IRS Publication 946, *How to Depreciate Property.*

Home-Based Business: Depreciation of your home (if you own the home) is part of the Home Expenses deduction, not deducted separately. See Home Expenses.

Design Costs

Most design costs, brochures, packages, and logos are deductible. Cost of trademarking a design may have to be amortized. See Trademarks.
   Expense category: Advertising.

Development

Product and business development expenses are usually deductible. See Research. Development expenses may also be eligible for the Research Tax Credit. See Tax Credits.
   Real estate developers: Predevelopment costs such as planning and design, building permits, engineering studies, landscape plans, and the like cannot be deducted currently but are depreciated.

Digital Currency

See Cryptocurrency.

Direct Costs

Direct costs of manufacturing or making crafts—materials, supplies, and paid labor that go into making the product—are part of inventory. See Inventory.

Direct Marketing
Direct Selling

Direct marketing and direct selling refer to a type of business, not to marketing expenses. If you are starting a direct marketing or direct selling business, see Startup Costs. If you are setting up a corporation, also see Organizational Costs.

Directors' Fees

Fees paid to corporate directors are deductible.
Expense category: Commissions and Fees.

Disability Insurance

Disability insurance covers a loss of income due to illness, injury, pregnancy, childbirth, or taking time off to care for a family member.

Disability insurance for self-employed people is not deductible. However, overhead insurance, which pays for business overhead expenses such as rent and utilities while you are recovering from illness or an injury, is deductible.

Expense category: For overhead insurance, Insurance.

Employers: Some states require employers to pay for disability insurance for their employees. This insurance is deductible if it is required by law. Also see Workers' Compensation Insurance.

Corporations: If your state requires you to carry disability insurance for yourself (as an employee of your business), the insurance is deductible.

Expense category: For employers, Employee Benefit Programs.

More information: For employers, IRS Publication 15-B, *Employer's Tax Guide to Fringe Benefits*.

In 1865 Congress authorized the position of assistant assessor and granted them "the power to increase a taxpayer's estimate of his income when it seemed to be an understatement." The assistant assessors were the first IRS auditors.

Disabled Access

The cost to purchase or modify equipment, buildings, or business grounds to meet the requirements of the Americans with Disabilities Act can be deducted or depreciated according to the deduction rules for each item. See Building Improvements. Also see Business Assets.

Disabled Access Tax Credit: Businesses that purchase equipment or devices, modify currently owned equipment or devices, or modify buildings or parking areas to make them more usable for disabled people are eligible for a Disabled Access Tax Credit. The maximum credit is $5,125. See Tax Credits. Businesses that gross over $1 million or have more than thirty employees are not eligible for this credit.

A Warning: This warning has nothing directly to do with tax deductions, but every business that has customers or clients who come to the premises or has fifteen or more employees is required to comply with the Americans with Disabilities Act. ADA rules are very specific, the requirements are lengthy, and the penalties can be steep. If you are out of compliance, you can be sued.

Disaster Losses

Deductible, but with special rules. See Casualty Losses.

Discounts

Regular list price $899.95. On sale today $14.95.

Discounts you give to customers are not an expense deduction. Discounts reduce your income. You show a lower gross income on your tax return.

Discount coupons for your customers are not an expense deduction, other than the cost of printing or distributing the coupons.

Discounts on items you purchase reduce the cost of the items being purchased. Discounts should not be recorded or deducted separately.

Expense category: Depends on what you are purchasing.

Employers: You can give discounts to employees and their families for anything your business makes or sells, tax free to them, as long as the discounted price is not below your cost. Employee discounts are recorded the same as discounts to customers.

Displays

Goods on display are considered inventory. See Inventory. Permanent display fixtures are business assets. See Business Assets. Display decorations can be deducted.

Expense category: For decorations, Supplies.

Dividends

Rebates to customers are sometimes called dividends. These rebates are deductible, not as an expense deduction but as a reduction to your income.

Expense category: Returns and Allowances.

Corporate dividends: When corporations distribute their profits to shareholders, these distributions are called dividends. Corporate dividends are not considered business expenses and are not deductible. Any costs associated with distributing dividends, such as bank or broker fees, are deductible.

Expense category: For costs and fees, Legal and Professional Services.

Domain Name

Expenses associated with acquiring, registering, and keeping a domain name are deductible (but see below). Also see Internet.

Expense category: Office Expenses.

Trademarks: Domain names that are trademarks are amortized over fifteen years. See Trademarks.

In 1913, Congress ratified the 16th Amendment to the Constitution establishing the federal income tax. In 1914, the Treasury Department unveiled Form 1040. According to the Internal Revenue Service, the number 1040 was a random selection. In Old England, Lady Godiva rode naked through the streets of Coventry to protest oppressive taxes. The year was 1040.

Donations

Businesses (other than C corporations) are not allowed a charitable deduction for donations to charities or community organizations. But charitable donations that result in publicity for the donor can often be deducted as an advertising or promotion expense.

I should point out that this interpretation of tax law (taking a promotion deduction for a charitable contribution) has been fought by the IRS for years. But the Tax Court has ruled in favor of the deduction several times, and the IRS has sometimes allowed it in audits. I suggest you read the Red Flag Warning below and then decide if you want to take the deduction.

Expense category: For cash donations, Advertising.

Merchandise: Donated inventory, such as a raffle prize for a fundraiser, or a food store donating food or beverages for a charity or community event, was deducted when the inventory was purchased (assuming your business is on the cash basis). There is no further deduction.

Gift certificates and gift cards: Cannot be deducted because no additional expense was incurred. Merchandise was deducted when it was purchased. If the gift is a service you provide, there is no tax deduction because you cannot deduct the cost of your own time. This is explained under Paying Yourself.

Percentage of sales donated: This deduction is the same as donating cash.

Expense category: Advertising.

Ads and sponsorships: An advertisement in a charitable organization's directory or event program, or sponsorship of an organization's team or event, is deductible. These expenses are not considered charitable donations. The IRS says they are legitimate promotional expenses. Instead of making a charitable donation that may or may not be deductible, place an ad or offer a sponsorship. As Father O'Malley said, "It's a win-win situation."

Expense category: Advertising.

Political donations are not deductible.

C Corporations: C corporations can deduct charitable contributions and donations as a charitable business deduction, if the charities have IRS charitable nonprofit status. C corporations can deduct up to 10% of their taxable income. C corporations that donate inventory to qualified charities can get a deduction for more than the cost of the inventory. They can deduct the cost plus half the difference between cost and regular sales price, up to twice the cost of the inventory.

Expense category: Charitable Contributions.

IRS Red Flag Audit Warning: The IRS, despite losing several times in Tax Court, still might challenge a business that deducts a donation as an advertising expense—if the IRS audits the business and if the auditor discovers the deduction. But since the deductions are included in advertising or other expenses, and not labeled charitable, the IRS is unlikely to spot the deductions. For me, if the Tax Court says the deduction is legitimate, so do I. Still, you may want to discuss this with an experienced accountant.

Father O'Malley answers the phone:
Is this Father O'Malley?
It is.
This is the IRS. Can you help us?
I can.
Do you know a Patrick Houlihan?
I do.
Is he a member of your congregation?
He is.
Did he donate $10,000 to the church?
He will.

Downloads

Downloaded music, apps, and publications, if for your business, are deductible. Downloaded software that you lease or subscribe to can be deducted currently. Downloaded software that you purchase can be deducted currently or can be amortized over three years. See Software.

Expense category: Software that you purchase (not subscribe to), Other Expenses. Other downloads, Office Expenses.

Down Payments

Down payments are treated the same as deposits. See Deposits.

Draw

Draw, partner, refers to drawing money out of your business. This is not an expense and is not a tax deduction.

When you are self-employed as a sole proprietor, partner in a partnership, or member (owner) of a limited liability company, you are not an employee of your business. You do not get a salary or a wage. If you want some money from your business, you "draw" it. That is, you just take it. See Paying Yourself.

Corporations: If you own a corporation, the rules are very different. You do not "draw" money, but you do pay yourself a salary, taxable as regular employee wages. Any money you take out of a corporation in excess of your salary is also not a draw. It is a taxable dividend. See Wages and Dividends.

Drilling

The cost of drilling and developing a water well can be depreciated over fifteen years.

Expense category: Depreciation.

More information: IRS Publication 946, *How to Depreciate Property*.

Oil and gas drilling: The costs of drilling oil and gas wells come under a complicated set of laws involving natural resources extraction that will require the help of an accountant with experience in this area.

Driveways

You can deduct the costs of maintaining a private road or driveway on your business property. The construction of a driveway is depreciated. See Depreciation. Also see Parking Lots.

Expense category: Repairs and Maintenance. For construction, Depreciation.

More information: IRS Publication 946, *How to Depreciate Property*.

Home-Based Business: A driveway is part of the Home Expenses deduction, not deducted separately. See Home Expenses.

Drones

Drones used for business can usually be deducted the year of purchase. See Business Assets.

You also have the option to depreciate these assets, write them off over seven years instead of deducting the cost all at once. See Depreciation to find out why you might want to choose this option.

Expense category: If you are depreciating the asset, Depreciation. If you are deducting the asset currently, either Depreciation or Other Expenses. See Business Assets.

More information: IRS Publication 946, *How to Depreciate Property*.

Drop Shipping

Drop shipping is a business arrangement where your business contracts with another business to warehouse and ship products to your customers for you. The drop shipper may be the manufacturer, importer, or wholesaler of the products, selling the products to you but shipping them to your customers for you; or the drop shipper may simply be a warehouse and shipping service.

Goods that you have drop shipped for you are considered inventory even though you never have them in stock. See Inventory.

Expense category: Inventory.

Drug Testing

Drug tests that are required by law are deductible. Drug tests for employees or independent contractors you hire, if not required by law, are deductible if they meet the IRS ordinary and necessary tests.

Expense category: Other Expenses.

Every year, Money.com asks fifty different tax preparers to prepare a 1040 form for a sample family. No two preparers arrived at the same result.

Dues

Dues to merchant associations and professional organizations are deductible. See Associations. Dues to service clubs such as Rotary and Lions are deductible.

Most club dues are not deductible, including business clubs.

Expense category: If deductible, Other Expenses.

Duties

Duties and all fees and taxes related to importing and exporting can be deducted, although these expenses can sometimes be added to the cost of the inventory being purchased or sold. You may want to talk to an accountant with export and import experience.

Expense category: For duties and tariffs, Taxes and Licenses. For non-government fees, Legal and Professional Services. If adding to the cost of the inventory, Inventory.

Education Expenses

The cost of education for self-employed individuals (sole proprietors, partners, LLC owners, and spouses in joint ventures) is deductible, if the education maintains or improves skills needed in your present work or is required to continue in your business or occupation.

Education expenses include tuition, registration fees, course fees, instructional material, textbooks, supplies, laboratory fees, travel between your business and the class location, and travel expenses while away from home overnight. Overnight travel is subject to limitations. See Travel.

Education expenses are not allowed if the education is required to meet minimum educational requirements of your business. Education expenses are not allowed if the education will qualify you for a new trade or business. The education needs to be related to a business you are already running, not a business you have not yet started.

Examples: A self-employed welder who takes a course in a new welding method can deduct the costs of the education. A self-employed dance teacher who also takes dance lessons can deduct the cost of the lessons. A professional can deduct the costs of continuing education in that profession. Any self-employed person can take a course in recordkeeping, or taxes, or computers, or most anything else related to your business, and deduct the cost.

Travel while you learn: You can even choose where you want to be educated. Sign up for a business seminar at a beach hotel in Hawaii, or on the cruise ship headed there, and write it off. Isn't that nice? You cannot, however, deduct travel itself as an education expense. You cannot deduct the cost of visiting stores in Paris, or New Orleans, or those charming little shops on Disneyland's Main Street.

Expense category: Other Expenses.

More information: IRS Publication 970, *Tax Benefits for Education.*

Partnerships and multi-owner LLCs: The business can pay for education expenses for the partners or the LLC owners and get a deduction. If the partners or LLC owners (not the businesses) pay for the education, the businesses can reimburse the partners or LLC owners and get the deduction, but only if you have an Accountable Reimbursement Plan, which is a written policy that the expenses are business related and that the expenses are substantiated (get receipts).

Employers: Employers can deduct, and employees can exclude from their income, the cost of job-related education expenses. Employers can also pay up to $5,250 annually for employee education expenses that are not job related (if the education involves sports, games, or hobbies, the education must be job related). To get the deduction, you are required to have a written educational assistance program. Payments in excess of $5,250 are considered taxable wages.

Corporations: You can deduct the cost of employment-related education for yourself. You cannot deduct the cost of education for yourself if the education is not related to your business. You do not qualify for the $5,250 deduction for employees.

Expense category: If tax free, Employee Benefit Programs. If taxable, Wages.

More information: IRS Publication 15-B, *Employer's Guide to Fringe Benefits*. IRS Publication 970, *Tax Benefits for Education*.

Scholarships: Scholarships you award (not to yourself) may be deductible. See Scholarships.

How many farmers does it take to change a light bulb? None. They get a tax subsidy for not changing them.

How many government employees does it take to change a light bulb? 45. One to change the bulb and 44 to handle the paperwork.

How many honest politicians does it take to change a light bulb? Both of them.

How many lobbyists does it take to change a light bulb? None. But by offering an all-expense-paid trip to the Bahamas they can get a Congressman to do it.

Electricity

Electricity and other utilities are deductible.

Expense category: Utilities.

Solar electric: If you purchase a solar electric system, you can deduct the cost or depreciate the system over five years. See Building Improvements for the rules.

Home-Based Business: Utilities are part of the Home Expenses deduction, not deducted separately. See Home Expenses.

Electronics

Electronic equipment and devices can be deducted the year purchased and first used in the business, or at your option, depreciated over five years. For details and special situations, see Business Assets.

Expense category: Depreciation or Other Expenses, depending on several factors. See Business Assets.

The Loophole Houdinis are devising ever more inventive ways to devise exotic tax shelters under the nose of the Internal Revenue Service.

—*BusinessWeek* magazine

It's not a loophole. It's the law.

—Tax accountant Joseph Lents

Employee Business Expenses

If an employer reimburses an employee for out-of-pocket business expenses, the employer is entitled to a tax deduction for the expenses.

However, there are some strict IRS rules about reimbursing employees and how the reimbursements affect employee wages. This also applies to owners of corporations. See Reimbursements.

Remember that a self-employed individual—sole proprietor, partner, or owner of an LLC—is not an employee of the business. Employee business expense reimbursements do not apply to self-employed individuals. Owners of corporations are employees of their businesses.

Expense category: Depends on actual expenses.

Employee Incentives

See Awards. Also see Fringe Benefits.

Employees

Wages and benefits you pay your employees are deductible. See Wages and Fringe Benefits. If you lease employees, see Temporary Help Agency. If you employ your spouse, see Spouse. If you employ your children, see Children on Payroll.

Expense category: Wages. For fringe benefits, Employee Benefit Programs.

More information: IRS Publication 15, *Employer's Tax Guide.*

Employment Agencies

Fees for employment agencies that charge you to find employees (such as executive search services) are deductible. Temporary help agency fees, for agencies that send their employees to work at your business, are also deductible, but see Temporary Help Agency for a warning.

Expense category: Legal and Professional Services.

Employment Tax Credits

A Work Opportunity Tax Credit and an Empowerment Zone Tax Credit are available for employers who hire certain disadvantaged employees. Both of these credits expire after 2025. See Tax Credits.

Expense category: Tax credits are taken on Form 1040, not on the business part of the tax return.

Employment Taxes

Deductible. See Payroll Taxes.

Expense category: Taxes and Licenses.

Empowerment Zone Tax Credit

Tax credit for hiring employees in certain low-income locations. Expires after 2025. See Tax Credits.

Expense category: Tax credits are taken on Form 1040, not on the business part of the tax return.

Energy

The cost of using energy in a business is usually deductible. Look up individual subjects.

Home-Based Business: Utilities are part of the Home Expenses deduction, not deducted separately. See Home Expenses.

Entertainment

Entertainment expenses are not deductible.

In some cases there is a fine line as to what is nondeductible entertainment, and what is not entertainment and therefore fully deductible. For example, a fashion show put on by a dress designer would not be considered entertainment, but a 100% deductible advertising expense. A party or lunch after the show, however, would be entertainment, not deductible.

Sometimes the term *promotion* is also called entertainment. But promotion expenses are fully deductible. You get to define your own expenses. The right choice of words will get you the right deduction.

Employers: A company party where all employees are invited is probably deductible. You should check with an accountant, as this deduction may be subject to disagreement.

Entertainers and entertainment business: The cost of entertainment that you provide is 100% deductible. This entertainment rule does not apply to you.

Environmental Remediation

See Contamination Cleanup.

Equipment

Equipment can be deducted the year purchased and first used in the business, or at your option, depreciated over five years. For details and special situations, see Business Assets.

Expense category: Depreciation or Other Expenses, depending on several factors. See Business Assets.

Estimated Taxes

Estimated tax payments are not deductible expenses.

Estimated tax payments are prepaid income and self-employment taxes that the IRS requires businesses to pay in advance if the estimated combined taxes are $1,000 or more ($500 or more for C corporations).

Exchange

Exchange, as in trade or barter, is a taxable transaction. Goods and services received in trade are deductible just like goods and services purchased with cash. See Barter/Trade.

Expense category: Varies depending on actual expenses.

Excise Tax

Federal excise taxes, if levied, are deductible.

The federal government imposes an excise tax, similar to a sales tax, on the manufacturers or sellers of some products and services. Highway trucks and trailers, tires, fuels, firearms, ammunition, tobacco, and alcohol are subject to excise tax. And tanning salons: a whopping 10% excise tax, part of the Affordable Care Act (Obamacare).

Expense category: Taxes and Licenses.

More information: IRS Publication 510, *Excise Taxes.*

State taxes: Some states call their corporate income tax an excise tax, and some states call their sales tax an excise tax or a general excise tax. These state taxes have different rules. See Income Tax and Sales Tax.

Marijuana businesses: State excise taxes are deductible. See "Marijuana businesses" in chapter 1.

Expense Accounts

Does anyone who owns a business actually have an expense account? Expense accounts per se are not deductible, but the actual expenses are deductible, depending on what the expenses are for. Also see Reimbursements.

Corporations: If you are an employee of your own corporation, see Employee Business Expenses.

Exporting

All duties, tariffs, fees, and taxes related to exporting can be deducted, although these expenses can sometimes be added to the cost of the inventory being sold. You may want to talk to an accountant with export and import experience.

Expense category: For duties and tariffs, Taxes and Licenses. For non-government fees, Legal and Professional Services. If adding to the cost of the inventory, Inventory.

Exterminator Service

Deductible.

Expense category: Other Expenses.

Home-Based Business: Exterminator costs are part of the Home Expenses deduction, not deducted separately. See Home Expenses.

Family

A family owned business, unless it is a corporation, does not get a deduction for any pay to the owner or owners of the business. See Paying Yourself.

Family employees: A spouse or a parent on your payroll—someone who is actually an employee of the business—is treated like any other employee, except a spouse and parents are not subject to Federal Unemployment (FUTA) tax (except corporations; see below). See Spouse and Parents on Payroll.

Children: If you hire your children, if they are under the age of eighteen, they may be exempt from income and payroll taxes. See Children on Payroll.

Corporations: Family members employed by your corporation are no different than any other employees, subject to all payroll taxes.

Expense category: Wages.

More Information: IRS Publication 15, *Employer's Tax Guide*.

The tax code has become so riddled with loopholes that tax avoidance has become a profit center of its own.

—*BusinessWeek* magazine

Attorneys and accountants should be pillars of our system of taxation, not the architects of its circumvention.

—Former IRS Commissioner Mark Everson

Farming

Most of the deductions in this book apply to farming businesses. Farmers also have additional, farming-only tax deductions.

For tax law, farming includes orchards, vineyards, plantations, ranches, and raising fish (though not fishing). Farming does not include plant and garden nurseries.

Expenses for planting, irrigation, livestock, feed, and agricultural supplies have their own tax rules, totally different than rules for nonfarming operations. Some farm-related buildings and structures have different depreciation rules than nonfarm structures.

There are enough rules specific to farming that I suggest you talk with an experienced accountant who regularly works with farms, vineyards, or whatever similar type of venture you are undertaking.

Expense category: There is no expense category called farming. Deductions depend on what is being deducted. Farmers do not file Schedule C. Farmers file Schedule F, Profit or Loss from Farming.

More information: IRS Publication 225, *Farmer's Tax Guide*.

Sideline farming: Many people have sideline farming income, which may or may not qualify them for the special deductions for farmers. Some deductions are available only to people who live and work on a farm or whose principal business is farming.

Home-based farming: Farms that are on the same property as the farmer's home are not considered home-based businesses and are not subject to the home-business limitations. However, farmers who have offices in their homes may qualify for the Home Expenses deduction for the office, in addition to any deductions for the farm.

Farm equipment: Mobile farm equipment can usually be deducted the year of purchase. See Business Assets.

You also have the option to depreciate these assets, write them off over five years instead of deducting the cost all at once. See Depreciation to find out why you might want to choose this option.

Expense category: For farm equipment, if you are depreciating the asset, Depreciation. If you are deducting the asset currently, either Depreciation or Other Expenses. See Business Assets.

More information: IRS Publication 946, *How to Depreciate Property.*

IRS Red Flag Audit Warning: "Weekend" farmers who claim losses on their farm operations are likely to face an audit, particularly if you have other substantial income. The IRS has always been suspicious of farming losses that offset other income and lower taxes. See "Hobby Income and Losses" in chapter 1.

The farmer is the man, the farmer is the man.
He lives on his credit until fall.
His pants are wearing thin, his condition is a sin,
But the taxes on the farmer feeds us all.

—Song from the Depression, author unknown

A man's respect for law and order exists in precise relationship to his paycheck.

—Congressman Adam Clayton Powell Jr. (1908–1972)

When you got nothing, you got nothing to lose.

—Jack Dawson Dylan, 1912, passenger on the *Titanic*
who won his passage in a poker game

Fees

Some fees are deductible, and some fees may have to be amortized over several years. Look up the individual fees.

FICA Tax

FICA tax for self-employed people is not deductible.

FICA stands for Federal Insurance Contributions Act. FICA tax is another name for Medicare and Social Security taxes. Self-employed people pay FICA taxes on their profits, but it is called self-employment tax. Self-employment tax is not deductible.

Employers: Employers deduct FICA taxes from employees' paychecks and also pay an employer's share. The employer's share is deductible.

Expense category: Taxes and Licenses (employer's portion only).

More information: IRS Publication 15, *Employer's Tax Guide*; IRS Publication 15-A, *Employer's Supplemental Tax Guide*.

Finance Charges

Finance charges are usually deductible, but sometimes with restrictions. See Interest.

Expense category: Interest.

Finders Fees

Finders fees, commissions, and the like are deductible.

Expense category: Commissions and Fees.

Fines

Fines and penalties for violation of the law are not deductible. Costs of compliance and restitution are deductible. Penalties for not meeting contract requirements, and any other fines or penalties that do not involve breaking the law, are deductible.

Expense category: Other Expenses.

A fine is a tax for doing something wrong. A tax is a fine for doing something right.

—Journalist Malcolm St. Pier

Fire Protection Systems

Inexpensive fire protection equipment such as a fire extinguisher can be deducted. See Business Assets. If the system is an integral part of a building, it can be deducted currently or depreciated along with the building. See Building Improvements.

Expense category: Depreciation (unless using the de minimis option; see Business Assets).

More information: IRS Publication 946, *How to Depreciate Property.*

Home-Based Business: Fire protection systems are part of the Home Expenses deduction, not deducted separately. See Home Expenses. A fire extinguisher in the business area can be deducted separately.

First Aid

Medical and emergency supplies are deductible.

Expense category: Office Expenses.

First-Year Write-Off

This refers to deducting business assets the year they are purchased. See Business Assets.

Fishermen and Fisherwomen

Self-employed fishermen and fisherwomen can take the same tax deductions as all other self-employed individuals. There are no special tax deduction rules. Everything in this book applies to you.

Fish farming businesses (not people who fish for a living) are considered farming businesses and come under special farming rules. See Farming.

Fish Farming

See Farming.

Fixed Assets

Fixed assets can be deducted the year purchased, or at your option, depreciated over several years. See Business Assets.

Fixed assets are machinery, equipment, furniture, fixtures, and most other assets the business owns. Some fixed assets are fixed in place, where the term originally came from (not fixed a million times and they still don't work), but fixed does not mean the assets are permanent parts of a building, bolted down, unmovable. This is an important distinction, because building components come under different rules than fixed assets. Fixed assets are also known as depreciable assets and business assets.

How can small businesses be so successful in the United States when our government appears so unfriendly and unhelpful?

—Former Senator Robert Dole

Fixed Costs

Most fixed costs are deductible.

Fixed costs refer to overhead, the dozens of large and small expenses you pay whether you are generating income or not. See Overhead.

Expense category: Varies depending on actual expenses.

Fixing-Up Expenses

Minor repairs to business property, buildings, and equipment are deductible as a current expense.

Expense category: Repairs and Maintenance.

Home-Based Business: Fixing-up costs are part of the Home Expenses deduction, not deducted separately. See Home Expenses.

Fixtures

Built-in building fixtures, those that came with the building, are depreciated as part of the cost of the building. Built-in building fixtures added after you acquire a building are deducted as building improvements. See Building Improvements.

Building fixtures that are not built-in can be deducted the year purchased and first used in the business, or at your option, depreciated over seven years. For details and special situations, see Business Assets.

Expense category: Depreciation or Other Expenses, depending on several factors. See Business Assets.

Home-Based Business: Built-in office fixtures are part of the Home Expenses deduction, not deducted separately. See Home Expenses.

I don't think government officials are against small business. They just have other priorities.

—Jere Glover, U.S. Small Business Administration

Flexible Spending Accounts

A flexible spending account is an employee fringe benefit plan. See Cafeteria Plan.

Floor Tax

Deductible.

Floor tax is a property tax on inventory, sometimes levied by local and state governments. Inventory sits on the floor, which is why the tax is some-

times called a floor tax. Inventory also sits on shelves, but the tax is never called a shelf tax. Whatever it is or isn't called, the tax is deductible.
Expense category: Taxes and Licenses.

Flowers

Yes, flowers are deductible: for the office, for the store, for your secretary, for a customer or client, for an office party.
Expense category: Office Expenses.

Food

Food samples available to the public are fully deductible. Food and beverages served at business-related events, such as a demonstration or exhibit, are deductible. Meals are partly deductible; see Meals.
Expense category: If samples of your goods, Inventory. If refreshments, Advertising.
Businesses that sell food: Food is deducted as inventory. See Inventory.

Foreign Expenses

Payments to companies and individuals outside the United States (sometimes called offshoring expenses) come under the same laws as payments to U.S. companies. Payments are fully deductible if they meet the deduction requirements.
Expense category: Varies depending on actual expenses.
Foreign income taxes: If you pay income taxes to a foreign country, you may be eligible for a tax credit. See Tax Credits.
More information: If self-employed, IRS Publication 514, *Foreign Tax Credit for Individuals.* If a corporation, Instructions for Form 1118, *Foreign Tax Credit—Corporations.*

Franchise Fees

Business franchise fees you pay to become a franchisee, licensee, or distributor may have to be amortized over fifteen years. You should check with an accountant who has franchise experience. Ongoing franchise fees are deductible.

Expense category: Other Expenses.

Franchise taxes: Do not confuse franchise fees with franchise taxes. They are completely different.

Franchise Taxes

Franchise taxes are deductible (generally; read on).

Franchise taxes are state taxes on corporations. Every state grants corporations what they call a franchise to do business in the state, for which the states charge an annual franchise tax. Some franchise taxes are annual fees, some take the form of an income tax. Corporations can deduct these taxes.

Unincorporated businesses: Most states do not impose franchise taxes on unincorporated businesses. But if your unincorporated business does pay a state franchise tax, it is deductible—if it is not an income tax. Some states call their income tax a franchise tax. Unincorporated businesses cannot deduct state income taxes on their federal tax returns. See Income Taxes.

Franchises: Don't confuse this franchise tax with franchise businesses (McDonald's, Holiday Inn, those kinds of businesses). The word *franchise* has two different meanings.

Expense category: Taxes and Licenses.

Fraud

If your business is defrauded, you may or may not be entitled to a tax deduction, depending on what kind of fraud actually occurred. See Casualty Losses.

Free Agents

Free agent is another term for independent contractor. Fees charged by free agents are deductible. See Independent Contractors.

Expense category: Contract Labor.

If you are a free agent, you are self-employed and are entitled to all the business deductions listed in this book.

Freelancers

Fees charged by freelancers and other independent professionals are deductible. See Independent Contractors.

Expense category: Contract Labor.

If you are a freelancer, you are self-employed and are entitled to all the business deductions listed in this book.

Freight

Freight and shipping costs on goods you sell are deductible. Weekly delivery service charges on a contract with UPS, FedEx, or other delivery service are deductible.

Expense category: Other Expenses.

Freight charges for business assets you are buying (machinery, equipment, furniture) should be added to the cost of the asset. See Business Assets. Freight charges for inventory you are buying are added to the cost of the inventory. See Inventory.

Fringe Benefits

Employers can deduct the cost of employee fringe benefits, with some exceptions and limits. Look up the individual items.

Expense category: Employee Benefit Programs.

More information: IRS Publication 15-A, *Employer's Supplemental Tax Guide*; IRS Publication 15-B, *Employer's Guide to Fringe Benefits*.

Also see Awards, Business Gifts, Dependent Care, Discounts, Education, Health Insurance, Life Insurance, Medical Expenses, Medical Savings Accounts, and Retirement Plans.

Fuel

All fuel costs are deductible. Fuel costs for cars and light trucks are deducted differently than fuel costs for large trucks and heavy-duty equipment. See Vehicles.

Expense category: Fuel for cars, vans, and small trucks: Car and Truck Expenses. Fuel for heavy-duty equipment and large trucks, also for boats and aircraft: Supplies. Fuel for heating: Utilities.

Furniture

Furniture can be deducted the year purchased and first used in the business, or at your option, depreciated over seven years. For details and special situations, see Business Assets.

Expense category: Depreciation or Other Expenses, depending on several factors. See Business Assets.

Home-Based Business: Furniture used for the business can be deducted in addition to and separate from the Home Expenses deduction. Furniture is not subject to the requirements and limitations of the Home Expenses deduction.

We don't pay taxes. Only the little people pay taxes.

—Billionaire hotel operator Leona Helmsley (1920–2007), who spent nineteen months in prison for federal tax evasion

---

Gambling Expenses

Generally, gambling expenses are not deductible as business expenses.

Professional gamblers who are in the business of gambling can deduct gambling expenses as business deductions, just like any other business, as long as the gambling is legal in your state. The deductions cannot exceed the income. You cannot show a loss.

IRS Red Flag Audit Alert: Claiming a deduction for gambling is inviting an audit. The IRS is very suspicious, often correctly, that gambling is really a hobby, not a business, and may also be an illegal activity. This is an area you may want to discuss with an experienced tax accountant (hopefully not with your criminal defense attorney).

Garbage and Recycling Service

Garbage service and other utilities are deductible.

Expense category: Utilities.

Home-Based Business: Utilities are part of the Home Expenses deduction, not deducted separately. See Home Expenses.

Gardening Expenses

Gardening, lawn care, and landscaping expenses are deductible. Hiring a gardener is deductible.

Expense category: Repairs and Maintenance.

Home-Based Business: If you take the flat-rate "safe harbor" deduction (explained under Home Expenses) you can ignore this warning because it does not apply to you. If you deduct actual expenses, the IRS prohibits a deduction for most gardening, landscaping, and lawn care expenses. Read the warning under Landscaping. It also applies to gardening.

General Business Credit

This is not one but several tax credits lumped under one heading. Look up individual credits. Also see Tax Credits.

Expense category: Tax credits are taken on Form 1040, not the business part of the tax return.

Gift Cards and Gift Certificates

There is no tax deduction for gift cards and gift certificates you sell or give away, other than the cost of producing the cards and certificates.

If the cards or certificates are redeemed for merchandise, you deduct the cost of the merchandise, unless you've already deducted the merchandise when you purchased it. See Inventory. If the cards or certificates are redeemed for services you provide, there is no tax deduction because the value of your own time is not a business expense. See Paying Yourself.

Purchased gift cards and certificates: If you pay for business goods or services using a gift card or gift certificate, you deduct what the card or certificate cost you, not what the product or service normally costs. If the card or certificate was a gift to you, you have no deduction because you did not pay anything.

Expense category: For items you purchase, the expense category depends on what was purchased. For the cost of producing cards and certificates, Office Expenses.

Accountants are boring. We hire people who have more personality.

—John T. Hewitt, founder, Jackson Hewitt Tax Service,
on hiring tax preparers without requiring them to have
backgrounds in tax preparation, reported in *Entrepreneur* magazine

---

Gifts

Gifts are deductible, with limits. See Business Gifts.

Gig Workers

If you hire gig workers (on-demand workers, sharing economy workers), they are independent contractors. You deduct the expense as you would for any other contract work. See Independent Contractors.

Expense category: Contract Labor.

If you are a gig worker, you are self-employed and eligible for every tax deduction in this book. Read "Gig Workers" in chapter 1. Also see Paying Yourself.

Goodwill
Going Concern Value

A portion of the purchase price of a business is often allocated to goodwill (going concern value) and can be amortized over fifteen years. See Buying a Business.

Goodwill has value because a successful business is worth more than a new business or a failing business. That intangible (and at times debatable) "worth" is also called blue sky.

Expense category: Other Expenses.

Graphic Design

Deductible, but see Design Costs.

Greeting Cards

Deductible. Good public relations too. People often ignore or never even look at email and internet greetings. Greeting cards are special.
Expense category: Office Expenses.

Grooming

Personal grooming expenses are not deductible, except when you're traveling away from home overnight on business. See Travel. Grooming expenses related to a show or other promotion are deductible.
Expense category: For a show, Other Expenses. If traveling, Travel.

Gross Receipts Tax

Gross receipts taxes are deductible.

A gross receipts tax is a tax on total business receipts—total sales, total income—before any deductions for expenses. There is no federal gross receipts tax. Some states and some cities have gross receipts taxes, but most don't.

Gross receipts tax is not income tax, although the IRS sometimes calls income tax a "tax on gross receipts" (just to confuse the issue).

Gross receipts tax is not sales tax. Some states call their sales tax a gross receipts tax, but the tax referred to here is not a sales tax. Sales tax is collected from your customers. Gross receipts taxes are paid out of your own pocket.
Expense category: Taxes and Licenses.

Group Health Insurance

The cost of a group health insurance plan for your employees is deductible. Former employees and families of employees can be included.

Expense category: Employee Benefit Programs.

More information: IRS Publication 15-B, *Employer's Tax Guide to Fringe Benefits.*

Coverage for yourself: If you are covered under a group insurance plan for your employees, you can deduct the cost for you and your family only if your business is a corporation. If you are self-employed (not incorporated), you are limited to the health insurance deductions for self-employed individuals. See Health Insurance.

Guaranteed Payments to Partners

Not deductible.

Some partnerships pay their partners a regular weekly or monthly paycheck, much like employee wages, what the IRS calls Guaranteed Payments to Partners. The payments, like all profits paid to partners, are not tax deductible. The payments come under the same rules as payments to sole proprietors, explained under Paying Yourself.

Health insurance: If your partnership pays health insurance for the partners, the payments are treated the same as guaranteed payments to partners. See Health Insurance.

Guard Dog

The cost of buying a guard dog can be deducted the year purchased and first used in the business, or at your option, depreciated over seven years. For details and special situations, see Business Assets.

Expense category: Depreciation or Other Expenses, depending on several factors. See Business Assets.

Care and feeding: Veterinary fees and the cost of feeding and maintaining the animal are deductible.

Expense: Office Expenses.

Guns

If having a gun is an ordinary and necessary expense of your business, firearms can be deducted the year purchased and first used in the business, or at your option, depreciated over seven years. For details and special situations, see Business Assets.

Expense category: Depreciation or Other Expenses, depending on several factors. See Business Assets.

Hair Care

See Personal Appearance.

Handicapped Access

See Disabled Access.

Handling Charges

Handling charges added to a shipping or freight bill are deducted like shipping costs. Handling charges for inventory you are buying are added to the cost of the inventory, not deducted separately. See Inventory. Handling charges for business assets you are buying (machinery, equipment, furniture) are added to the cost of the asset. See Business Assets.

It's very hard to tell struggling small businesses why they should be honest and pay their taxes when the big companies are hiring lobbyists to get out of their tax liability.

—Dean Baker, Director, Center for Economic Policy and Research

---

Hazardous Material Disposal

See Contamination Cleanup.

Health Benefits

See Health Insurance and Medical Expenses.

Health Insurance

Sole proprietors, partners in partnerships, members of LLCs, and owners of S corporations can get a tax deduction for the cost of health insurance for themselves and their spouses and dependents. There are some restrictions and limits.

The health insurance deduction may not exceed the net profit from your business. The deduction is not allowed if you are eligible for employer-paid health insurance through your own employer (if you have another job) or through your spouse's employer.

To get the health insurance deduction, the insurance plan must be either in the name of the business or in the name of the self-employed individual. If your spouse is shown as the main insured on your policy, ask your insurance company to change the name on the policy. The change should not affect your coverage or premiums.

I also suggest you pay the health insurance premiums from your business bank account, even if the policy is not in the business's name. Some tax experts have stated that this is an IRS requirement. I've never found this requirement in the IRS code or any IRS notices or publications, but it certainly will help in the unlikely chance that an IRS auditor might challenge the deduction. If you don't have a business bank account, or if you pay by credit card, take the deduction anyway and don't worry about it.

Expense category: The deduction is taken on your 1040 return, not on Schedule C. The deduction is not a business expense, is not deducted on the business part of your tax return, and does not reduce your business profit.

More information: IRS Publication 334, *Tax Guide for Small Business.*

Medical expenses: You cannot take this deduction for medical expenses, just insurance. Medical expenses are not deductible. See Medical Expenses.

Partnerships: The health insurance policy can be purchased by the partners themselves or by the partnership. But if the partners purchase the policies, the partnership is required to reimburse the partners and report the reimbursement as guaranteed payments to partners on the partnership tax return.

S corporations: The health insurance policy can be purchased by the owner-employees of the corporation or by the corporation itself. But if the owners purchase the policies, the corporation is required to reimburse the owners. In both situations, the corporation reports the cost of the premiums as taxable wages to the owner-employees.

Medicare: Medicare premiums—the insurance premiums you pay when you are on Medicare—are considered health insurance. Medicare tax that you pay as part of your self-employment tax is considered health insurance and is deductible (but see Medicare for a warning).

Long term care insurance: Premiums for long term care insurance can be included as part of the above health insurance deduction. Long term care insurance, however, is subject to a dollar limitation, which the IRS changes from year to year, and which varies depending on your age. There is no dollar limitation on regular health insurance. For long term care limits, see IRS Publication 535, *Business Expenses*.

Disability insurance: Insurance that pays you for lost earnings if you are disabled is not considered health insurance and is not deductible.

Employers: Health and long term care insurance for your employees, their spouses, and dependents are 100% deductible as a business expense. Employers can also reimburse employees for actual medical expenses for the employees and employees' families: doctor bills, hospitals, prescriptions, lab tests, and many other medical expenses. The employer gets a full deduction, and the payments are not taxable to the employees. Be careful, however, not to reimburse employees for the cost of health insurance they themselves purchase. The reimbursement may be considered taxable wages. In addition to the deductions, employers with twenty-five or fewer full-time workers may also be eligible for a Small Business Health Care Tax Credit. See Tax Credits.

Spouse on payroll: If your spouse is an employee of your business, on the payroll with regular employee payroll deductions, your spouse *and* family (i.e., you and your children) are eligible for full employee health benefits, both health insurance and actual medical expenses, and the cost is fully deductible as a business expense. You come under the 100% deductible employee health insurance rules, not the self-employment insurance rules, a big tax savings. To get this deduction, all your employees (if you have other employees) must be covered. Also, according to a recent IRS court case, the spouse must be the primary insured on the policy, and premiums must be paid from the business checking account, assuming you have a business checking account. If you don't, just pay however you can and don't worry about it.

IRS Red Flag Audit Warning: Putting your spouse on the payroll and deducting your entire family's health insurance is a loophole in the tax law that the IRS is suspicious of. The IRS has often challenged the deduction on the grounds that the spouse is not really an employee or is only doing minimal work, and is only on the payroll to get the health coverage. The

IRS considers the cost of the health benefits to be "unreasonable compensation"; that is, more money than is reasonable for the amount and type of work your spouse is doing. You may want to talk to an accountant familiar with this deduction.

C corporations: If you are an employee of your own C corporation (not S corporation), you, your spouse, and dependents are eligible for full employee medical coverage, but only if all your employees are covered.

Expense category: Employee Benefit Programs.

More information: IRS Publication 15-B, *Employer's Guide to Fringe Benefits.*

Heating

Heating and other utilities are deductible.

Expense category: Utilities.

Garbage and recycling service: Garbage service and other utilities are deductible.

Expense category: Utilities.

Home-Based Business: Utilities are part of the Home Expenses deduction, not deducted separately. See Home Expenses.

Highway Use Tax

The highway use tax is an excise tax on truckers. It is deductible.

Expense category: Taxes and Licenses.

Hobby Expenses

Hobbies are not businesses. Hobby expenses are not deductible. But that doesn't mean you can't turn your hobby into a real, legitimate write-off-the-expenses business. Thousands of successful businesses started out as hobbies. See "Hobby Income and Losses" in chapter 1.

Holiday Cards

Deductible.

Christmas or Season's Greetings cards are always noticed and appreciated. One company I did business with always sent their customers a Thanksgiving card, the only one I ever got. I always remembered them because of the card. But then, I once had a dentist who sent his patients birthday cards. Who wants to hear from your dentist—on your birthday!
Expense category: Office Expenses.

There is nobody in this country who got rich on his own. Nobody. You built a factory out there, good for you. But, I want to be clear: You moved your goods to market on the roads the rest of us paid for. You hired workers the rest of us paid to educate. You were safe in your factory because of police forces and fire fighters the rest of us paid for. You built a factory and it turned into something terrific. God bless. Keep a big hunk of it. But part of the underlying social contract is you take a hunk of that and pay forward for the next kid who comes along.

—U.S. Senator Elizabeth Warren

Home Expenses
Business Use of Your Home

Business use of a home is deductible—not just for home businesses, but for any business using the home for any business-related activity—as long as you are careful to follow the rules, which are lengthy but not difficult.

This home expense deduction is for the space in your home that is used for business. Anyone who has a business office in the home, sees customers in the home, does business-related work at home, or has business storage at home may be eligible for this deduction.

The deduction, often called the home office deduction, is not just for an office in the home. It is for any business space—office, workshop, studio, warehouse, store, showroom—and the expenses directly related to the space including rent or depreciation, utilities, insurance, property taxes, maintenance, home repairs, remodeling, air-conditioning, painting, and decorating: most everything associated with the office itself, except office furniture and equipment, which are deducted separately and do not come under these home expense rules; see Business Assets.

The term *home* includes a house, apartment, loft, condominium, trailer, mobile home, or boat if you are living on it. The term also includes any separate structure that is part of your residence such as a garage, shop, or other building.

Failure to qualify for this home deduction doesn't prohibit you from operating your business out of your home. It only means that one possibly large expense, the cost of the space itself, is not deductible. You can still deduct all legitimate business expenses other than those directly related to the business space.

The home expense rules apply to sole proprietors, spousal partnerships, and one-owner LLCs. Partnerships, corporations, and multi-owner LLCs may be able to claim a home expense deduction, depending on several factors (covered below).

The requirements:

To be eligible for the home deduction, the business space (the office, workshop, studio, or whatever you are using the building for) needs to meet two basic rules: (1) a principal place of business, and (2) regular and exclusive use.

A principal place of business. Your home must meet at least one of the following four requirements. Any one of the four qualifies you:

1. The home must be your principal place of business, defined by the IRS as "the most important, consequential, or influential location."
2. The home must be used regularly, not just occasionally, by your customers or clients.
3. The home must be used regularly to generate sales, such as making calls and preparing estimates.
4. The home must be the sole fixed location where you conduct substantial administrative or management activities for the business: where you do your paperwork or your research, or order supplies, or schedule appointments. You don't have to do all your administrative or management work at home, but it should be the main location for these activities.

Regular and exclusive use. A specific part of your home must be used regularly and exclusively for business. It can be a separate room or even part of a room, as long as it is used for the business and nothing else. Period. No television in the office. No personal paperwork at the desk. (No games on the computer?) The business area can't double as a guest room, kid's room, or anything else, even when you are not working.

There are two exceptions to the exclusive rule: (1) If your home is your sole location for a retail sales business and if you regularly store your inventory or your samples in your home, the expense of maintaining the storage area is deductible even if it isn't exclusive use of the space. (2) If you operate a licensed day care facility in your home, you do not have to use the space exclusively for business.

Taking the deduction:

There are two options for taking a home deduction. You can deduct actual expenses, or you can take a standard flat-rate deduction.

Deducting actual expenses involves keeping detailed records of expenses, calculating percentage of use, and filing an additional tax form, Form 8829, Expenses for Business Use of Your Home. Most important, if it is a home you own, you may have possible tax problems when you sell the home (covered below).

By comparison, the flat-rate deduction (the IRS calls it the Safe Harbor Method) is simple to figure, does not require Form 8829, and eliminates any tax complications when you sell your home.

Although the flat-rate deduction is much easier to calculate and requires much less paperwork than using actual expenses, it probably will result in a lower deduction amount. Also, if your business is showing a loss, the flat-rate deduction has some limitations (covered below).

You can calculate the home deduction both ways and then decide which will give you the biggest deduction and the fewest hassles. Once you select a method, you are not stuck with it for future years. You can use one method one year, and the other method the next year if you want.

Flat-rate deduction: The deduction is $5 per square foot of business space, up to a maximum of 300 square feet. So the maximum annual flat-rate deduction is $1,500. This flat-rate option is in lieu of deducting actual expenses for the space itself. Office furniture and equipment, as well as all other normal business expenses other than those directly related to the space, are deductible in addition to the flat rate.

Business loss: The flat-rate deduction cannot exceed the net profit from your business. You can take the flat-rate deduction only up to the point your profit drops to zero. If your business is already showing a loss, you cannot take the deduction at all. Any unused part of the flat-rate deduction cannot be applied to future years. Businesses with losses probably should use the actual-expense option, which allows the deduction to be carried forward to future years if the business is showing a loss.

More than one business: If you have more than one business, the 300-square-foot maximum is for all businesses combined. If a spouse or housemate also has a business, that person is also entitled to a $5-per-square-foot deduction for up to 300 square feet, but not for the same portion of the home. If two people share the same space, the combined deduction cannot be more than $5 per square foot.

Deducting actual expenses: If you choose this option, deductible expenses include a percentage of your rent if you rent your home, or a percentage of the depreciation if you own your home, and an equal percentage of home utilities, property tax, building maintenance and repairs, security system, garbage pickup, mortgage interest, insurance, and any other building-related expenses. You can determine the percentage based on square footage or if the rooms in your home are about the same size, by the number of rooms.

Expenses that are only for the business, such as office cleaning, painting the office, air-conditioning, decorating, or buying extra insurance coverage are 100% deductible if they are 100% for the business; you do not prorate them.

Landscaping: The only exceptions to the deductions are for landscaping and lawn care, which the IRS says are not deductible, although the Tax Court has overruled the IRS several times. See Landscaping for more information.

Business loss: If your business shows a loss, some of your home expenses are not deductible this year. You may deduct interest and property taxes on the home, regardless of profit or loss. But the remaining home expenses may be deducted this year only if your business shows a profit. Any expenses you cannot deduct due to this limitation can be carried forward and deducted in future years.

Tax trap for homeowners: If you are deducting actual expenses, you will run into tax complications when you sell your house. Any depreciation you were allowed must be "recaptured." This means that you add up all the depreciation during all the years you used your home for business, and pay tax on that depreciation when you sell the house. This is a complicated law, and an unwelcome tax, that you can avoid by taking the flat-rate deduction.

Another tax trap: If the business is located in a separate structure on the same property as your home (such as a detached garage or barn, even a structure specially built to house your business) when you sell your home, the building housing the business is not eligible for the tax exemption homeowners get when they sell their homes. Any profit on the sale of the separate business structure is fully taxable. This quirk in the law applies only to separate structures, not to a business located inside your main residence or in an attached garage. This problem can be avoided by taking the flat-rate deduction.

More rules:

Part-time business: If you operate a business part-time on a regular basis, you can take the full Home Expense deduction. You do not have to prorate the expenses for time or days worked. The IRS does not define part-time nor does it define regular basis, but the IRS does say that "incidental" or "occasional" business use does not qualify. I'm sure you can figure a way to set up your business work schedule to qualify for this deduction. This part-time rule does NOT apply to part-year or seasonal businesses. See below.

Part-year business: If you operate a business for only part of a year— if you operate a seasonal business or a pop-up business, or if you start or close the business during the year—you prorate the deduction for how many months of the year the business is in operation. Any month that you operate a business for fifteen or more days can be counted as a full month.

More than one location: If your business is also operated out of another location, such as a store, you are still eligible for a home deduction in addition to the cost of renting the store, if the home meets the above requirements.

More than one business: You can have a separate principal place of business for each trade or business you operate. You can have a home-based business getting the home office deduction, and a separate business outside the home. If you have more than one home-based business, both using the same home space, you must split the deduction, half (or some other percentage split) for each business.

More than one home: A home deduction is allowed only for your principal place of business, which cannot be two different places. You can't run a business out of two homes and get two home deductions. If you move to a new home during the year, you can have two principal places of business for different parts of the year, but curiously, the IRS will not allow you to take the flat-rate deduction. The IRS will allow you to deduct actual expenses on both homes, part of the year on one home and part on the other. If you are operating two different businesses out of two different homes, you can take the home deduction for each business. You now have two principal places of business independent of each other. (Sorry, I didn't make these rules.)

Renting your home to your business: Some business owners rent their home to their business and take a business deduction for the rent expense. This is not usually a good idea. While this gives your business a tax deduction, it saddles you with taxable rental income and a possible loss of your home tax exemption.

Child care and day care businesses: The home deduction is allowed only if your business is officially licensed as a child care or day care business (unless your business is exempt from state licensing rules) and your business cares for children, or people age sixty-five or older, or people who are unable to care for themselves.

Only the space used for the care activities can be deducted, and only for the days used. Space used for part of a day is eligible for a full-day deduction. No need to prorate it for hours of use. Child care and day care businesses are exempt from the exclusive use rule. You get a full deduction for rooms used in your business even if they are also used for nonbusiness purposes.

Lodging businesses: If you operate a separate hotel or inn on your property (a separate structure from your home), it is not considered a home business. You do not have to meet the Home Expenses rules.

If you operate a lodging business inside your home—bed-and-breakfast, boardinghouse, or rooming house, or if you rent out rooms—only the portion of the home used exclusively for the business can be deducted. Shared space such as a dining room and your own private space cannot be deducted.

Renting out rooms through online platforms such as Airbnb comes under the same rules as boardinghouses and bed-and-breakfasts, but only if the income qualifies as self-employment income. See the discussion of rental income in chapter 1.

Partnerships, corporations, and multi-owner LLCs cannot take the Home Expenses deduction, not directly anyway. The owner of the business (the person whose home is being used for business) can get a reimbursement from the business for the owner's home expenses, and then the business could deduct the reimbursement as a business expense.

The IRS requires that this type of arrangement have an Accountable Reimbursement Plan, which is a written policy that the expenses are business related and that the expenses are substantiated (you have receipts). Also, the partnership or LLC agreement or the corporate bylaws should include a clause requiring you to use your home for business. If your current agreement or bylaws do not include such a statement, amend them to include this requirement. If you do not have the reimbursement plan and the written agreements, your business cannot take the deduction.

Expense category: Expenses for Business Use of Your Home.

More information: IRS Publication 587, *Business Use of Your Home.*

Tax laws are complicated and unfriendly. Figuring out whether a home office can be deducted is a more difficult question than balancing the national budget. So most of us just give up and pay the full tax.

—Tom Person, Laughing Bear Publishing, Houston, Texas

Homeowner Fees/Associations

If you are eligible for the Home Expenses deduction explained above, and if you are deducting actual expenses, a percentage of your homeowner fees is deductible as part of that deduction. If you are taking the flat-rate deduction, these fees are included as part of the deduction, and no additional deduction is allowed.

Housing Allowances

Housing allowances provided by an employer to employees are a tax-deductible expense, if the lodging meets the IRS's ordinary and necessary tests.

The allowance, however, is taxable to the employees as wages unless it meets three additional requirements: (1) the lodging is on the employer's business premises, (2) the lodging is for the employer's convenience, and (3) the lodging is required as a condition of employment. If these three requirements are met, the housing is tax free for the employees.

Expense category: Employee Benefit Programs.

More information: IRS Publication 15-B, *Employer's Tax Guide to Fringe Benefits.*

HR 10 Plan

Another name for a Keogh retirement plan, also known as a Qualified Plan. See Retirement Plans.

Expense category: Deducted on the 1040 form.

More information: IRS Publication 560, *Retirement Plans for Small Business.*

Husband on Payroll

See Spouse.

Illegal Expenses

Not all outlaws are criminals, but it's illegal to take a deduction for illegal expenses. As Nancy Reagan said, Just say no . . . deduction allowed.

Importing

All fees and taxes related to importing can be deducted, although these expenses can sometimes be added to the cost of the inventory being purchased. You may want to talk to an accountant with export and import experience.

Expense category: For duties and tariffs, Taxes and Licenses. For non-government fees, Legal and Professional Services. If adding to the cost of the inventory, Inventory.

I love it whenever Congress passes tax changes. We grow and continue to expand.

—John Hewitt, Founder and CEO, Liberty Tax Service

Improvements

See Building Improvements.

Incentives

Incentive payments to customers, vendors, and other nonemployees are deductible, within limits. See Prizes.

Expense category: Depends on what the payments are for.

Employers: Incentive payments to employees, other than token non-monetary gifts, are considered wages, taxable to the employee and subject to regular payroll taxes. However, employees can receive employee achievement awards that are not considered taxable wages. See Awards.

Incidental Materials and Supplies

Materials and supplies (basically the same thing) that cost $2,500 or less—what the IRS calls Incidental Materials and Supplies—are deducted when purchased.

Expense category: For office supplies, Office Expenses. For other deductible supplies, Supplies.

Supplies that cost more than $2,500 come under a different rule. See Non-incidental Materials and Supplies.

Income Deduction

See Qualified Business Income Deduction.

Income Taxes

Federal income taxes are not deductible. State and local income taxes are not deductible for sole proprietorships, partnerships, S corporations, or LLCs, but are deductible for C corporations.

Expense category: For C corporations only, Taxes and Licenses.

State tax returns: Some states allow businesses, both corporations and noncorporations, to deduct federal income taxes (and sometimes local income taxes) on their state income tax returns.

IRS Service Center, Odgen, Utah

Foreign income taxes: If you pay income taxes to a foreign country, you may be eligible for a tax credit. See Tax Credits.

More information: For corporations, Instructions for Form 1118, *Foreign Tax Credit.* For self-employed people, IRS Publication 514, *Foreign Tax Credit for Individuals.*

Every time lawmakers try to simplify the code, tax laws just get more complicated.

—Tax analyst Paula Gada, CCH Tax Publications

I hold in my hand 1,379 pages of tax simplification.

—Congressman Del Latta, holding a copy of the most recent tax revisions

---

Incorporation Fees

If you are incorporating an existing business, fees to incorporate the business are deductible. If you are incorporating a new business, the deductions are limited. See Organizational Costs.

Expense category: Taxes and Licenses.

In 1864 Mark Twain paid $36.82 in income tax, plus a $3.12 late filing fine.

Independent Contractors

The cost of hiring an independent contractor is deductible.

Independent contractors are people who sell their services on a contract basis, usually for a temporary time or for a specific project. Independent contractors are self-employed, in business for themselves.

The term *contractor* has a much broader meaning in tax law than just building contractors and similar trades. Most freelancers, consultants, free agents, and self-employed professionals are independent contractors. On-demand workers (gig workers) are independent contractors. Independent contractors are also called outside contractors (not because they work outdoors, but because they work outside the regular employment system).

Independent contractors are not employees. Employment laws and regulations do not apply to independent contractors. When you hire an independent contractor, you do not withhold taxes, pay employment taxes, provide health insurance, or file payroll tax returns. When you hire an independent contractor, you pay the contractor his or her fee in full. The fee is fully deductible.

Expense category: Contract Labor.

IRS Red Flag Audit Warning: Businesses and the IRS have been arguing for years over who should be classified as an employee and who should be classified as an independent contractor. There are serious risks to businesses that misclassify employees as independent contractors, and significant costs may be at stake. I devote an entire chapter in my book *Small Time Operator* to the differences between independent contractors and employees. If you are unsure how to classify a worker, get advice from an experienced accountant.

Indirect Costs (Manufacturing)

The deduction for indirect manufacturing costs depends on what the costs are for.

Inventory that is produced by manufacturers and crafts businesses has two components: direct costs, which are the materials that go into the products, the shipping or freight costs to deliver the inventory to the manufacturer, and paid labor to produce the products; and indirect costs, all of the other expenses incurred to manufacture a product, including the cost of the building, utilities, manufacturing equipment and machinery, maintenance, and anything else involved in production.

Direct costs are deducted as part of Inventory. See Inventory. Indirect costs are deducted separately, according to the tax laws for each cost. Look up each component (buildings, machinery, utilities, etc.) to determine how to deduct them.

Individual Retirement Arrangement (IRA)

Contributing to an IRA, which is a tax-deferred retirement plan for individuals, is not a deductible business expense. See Retirement Plans.

Expense category: Deducted on the 1040 form, not on the business part of the tax return.

Employers cannot deduct contributions to an employee's IRA but can deduct contributions to an employee's SEP-IRA, which is different than an IRA. See Retirement Plans.

If the IRS had to prepare its own tax return, with the many problems we have found during our financial statement audits of the IRS, it would not pass the scrutiny of an IRS audit.

—Gregory Holloway, U.S. General Accounting Office

The IRS has been using an old system of accounting that is simply not auditable.

—IRS Chief Financial Officer Morgan Kinghorn

Installation Costs

Minor installation costs can be deducted currently. The cost to install machinery or equipment, if significant, is added to the cost of the asset being installed, not deducted separately. See Business Assets.

Expense category: If deducting currently, Other Expenses.

Installment Purchases

If you are buying business assets such as buildings, equipment, vehicles, furniture, fixtures, and machinery, you can deduct or depreciate the full cost, even though you haven't paid all of it yet. This is allowed even if you are on the cash method of accounting. See Business Assets.

Insurance

Most business insurance premiums are deductible, though with several exceptions.

For a price, there is insurance for just about everything: fire, extended coverage, earthquake, riot, flood, earth movement, lightning, glass breakage, general liability, fire, legal liability, property damage liability, products liability, malpractice, errors and omissions, professional liability, theft, business interruption, workers' compensation, medical, vehicle, environmental impairment, pollution liability, vandalism and malicious mischief, patent protection, disability, key person life insurance, equipment breakdown, tax audit insurance, credit insurance for accounts receivable, copyright insurance, export insurance, computer meltdown insurance, cyber-insurance if you are hacked, employment practices insurance, bad weather insurance (if the weather ruins an outdoor event), and—a sad sign of the times—sexual harassment insurance. There's even insurance that insures your insurance, called umbrella insurance, in case you aren't covered when you thought you were.

Expense category: Insurance.

Exceptions:

Prepaid insurance: Prepaid insurance, if it does not extend beyond twelve months, is deductible when paid. Prepaid insurance beyond twelve months is prorated between years.

Vehicle insurance: Deductible only if you don't take the Standard Mileage Rate. See Vehicles.

Workers' compensation insurance: Deductible for your employees. For self-employed individuals, workers' compensation premiums for yourself are deductible only if your state requires you to cover yourself. If your own coverage is not required by state law, it is not deductible.

Disability insurance: Deductible for your employees. Disability insurance for yourself is not deductible unless you are an employee of your corporation.

Life insurance: Self-employed individuals cannot deduct the cost of life insurance on themselves. Premiums for group term life insurance paid by an employer on behalf of employees are deductible, but only if the employer is not a beneficiary. If coverage exceeds $50,000, the premiums are added to the employee's compensation as additional wages, subject to payroll taxes.

Business interruption insurance: Insurance that covers business overhead while you are disabled or unable to work is deductible. Insurance that pays you for lost earnings while you are disabled or unable to work is not deductible.

Health insurance: Health insurance has so many rules, it has its own category. See Health Insurance.

Self-insurance: Some businesses, in lieu of buying insurance, set aside funds to cover possible losses such as fire or theft or a liability claim against the business. Some people call these funds a "reserve." The money set aside or put into a reserve is not considered a business expense and is not tax deductible.

Home-Based Business: Homeowner insurance and renter insurance are part of the Home Expenses deduction, not deducted separately. See Home Expenses.

Blaming the IRS is a lot like blaming the doctor whose patient has an incurable disease. Tax reform, not IRS bashing, is the only way to liberate the American people from a system that is grotesquely burdensome.

—Former IRS Commissioner Fred Goldberg

Intangibles
Intellectual Property

Most intangible assets (also called intellectual property) are amortized over a period of years, but some intangibles can be deducted currently.

Intangible assets are business assets you cannot see such as copyrights, trademarks, patents, and goodwill. Some trademark expenses can be written off when paid. Individual copyrights are so inexpensive, most businesses deduct them when paid. Software is considered an intangible, but software can be deducted currently or can be amortized over three years; see Software. Look up individual items for specific rules.

Expense category: Other Expenses.

Interest Expense

Interest paid on business debts, interest on credit card purchases, and interest on purchases of business assets is deductible, with a few important exceptions.

Expense category: Interest. If added to the cost of real estate or equipment, Depreciation.

Construction: Interest on loans to construct real estate are capitalized, added to the cost of the property, and depreciated. See Depreciation.

Points: Points and other loan origination fees are deductible, but the deduction is spread out over the length of the loan.

Back taxes: Interest on back taxes is not deductible, except for corporations, even if the back taxes are business related.

Personal loans: Interest on a personal loan is deductible as a business expense if the loan was used for your business. Be sure to keep good records showing that the money was really put into your business.

Real estate and equipment: Interest on some real estate and equipment purchases can, at your option, be capitalized (added to the cost of the building or equipment) and depreciated over a period of years rather than deducted currently. This may be advantageous if you are just starting out in business and do not need the immediate tax deduction. I suggest you discuss this with an experienced accountant.

Prepaid: The IRS says that prepaid interest is not deductible until the year it applies to, even for cash method businesses.

Buying a business: If you borrow money to purchase an existing business, the laws can get complicated. Part of the interest may be deductible as a current business expense, but part may have to be capitalized, depending on what you are purchasing (assets or corporate stock). You will probably need an experienced accountant's help.

Corporations: If you get a personal loan to purchase business assets for your corporation, the interest is not deductible as a business expense. If the corporation itself borrows the money, the interest is deductible. If you are a personal guarantor of the loan, the corporation can deduct the interest as long as the loan is in the corporation's name.

Internet Access

The cost of internet access is fully deductible if used only for business. If used partly for business, you prorate the cost and deduct only the business portion. Also see Domain Name and Website.

Expense category: Office Expenses.

The IRS is using social networking as a tax enforcement tool by having their revenue agents track down tax evaders on social media.

—Kiplinger Tax Letter

Inventory

Inventory can be deducted when purchased, or at your option, deducted when sold. For any business with inventory, this is a major tax deduction, probably the biggest one on your tax return. Which method you select can have a significant impact on the taxes you pay.

Inventory is merchandise that you sell or manufacture. Inventory also includes repair parts and manufacturing parts, and materials and supplies that go into manufacturing or repairing a product.

The two deduction options depend on how you record your expenses, using the cash accounting method or the accrual accounting method.

Cash accounting: Businesses using the cash accounting method, which most small businesses use, deduct the cost of inventory when purchased.

Accrual accounting: Businesses using accrual accounting, which almost no small businesses use, deduct the cost of inventory when sold (or disposed of), not when you buy it. If you choose this accrual accounting option, the amount you deduct every year is determined by a calculation called "cost of goods sold." To learn how to make the calculation, see Cost of Goods Sold.

Which method should you use?: Normally, most businesses want to write off expenses when paid, take the full deduction the current year, and reduce taxable income and taxes. But with inventory, this may not be the best choice.

If you regularly have little or no inventory on hand at the end of the year, the difference in the two options is insignificant. Use the cash accounting option, deduct the inventory when you purchase it, and keep the accounting simple.

But if you have a large inventory on hand at the end of the year, you may have a significant tax savings by postponing the deduction until future years.

Businesses with large inventories: For businesses with substantial inventories, such as retail stores full of merchandise and manufacturers with warehouses full of parts, how you deduct your inventory—under the cash method, deducting the cost when you make the purchase, or under the accrual method, deducting the cost when you sell the goods—will have a dramatic impact on your profit or loss for the year and on the income taxes you'll pay.

For example, let's say you own a retail store and you purchase $50,000 worth of goods to stock the store. And let's say that during the year, you sold $25,000 of those goods and still have $25,000 on hand at December 31. Do you write off the entire $50,000 this year (using the cash method)? Or do you only deduct the $25,000 cost of what you sold this year, writing off the $25,000 balance next year or whenever you sell the goods (using the accrual method)?

That decision will affect both this year's and next year's profit and taxes. If you deduct the entire $50,000 this year, you may find that you have more tax deductions than you need to minimize this year's taxes. You may benefit by postponing part of the deduction (in our example, the $25,000 of goods on hand at the end of the year) and take the deduction next year, to offset next year's income.

Again, this is an important decision. A lot of tax money may be at stake. Once you choose a method, you cannot switch to the other method without approval from the IRS.

If you choose the accrual method, see Cost of Goods Sold to learn how to determine the deductible amount for this year and future years.

Expense category: Inventory.

More information: IRS Publication 538, *Accounting Periods and Methods.*

New businesses: If you are starting a new business and already have inventory on hand that you will be putting into the business, inventory you purchased before going into business, you can add the cost of that inventory (or the market value if less than cost) to the current year's purchases, even though you didn't buy it this year, and include it as part of your inventory deduction.

Non-incidental materials and supplies: The IRS deduction rules for inventory refer to an expense called non-incidental materials and supplies, which you do not need to be concerned with. But it has confused many people, particularly those who read the IRS instructions for Schedule C. This is the story:

A massive tax law passed a few years ago dramatically rewrote the rules for deducting inventory. Under the new law, you can deduct inventory under the same rules as "non-incidental materials and supplies," a little-known tax category that allows a tax deduction only when the materials or supplies are "first used or consumed."

Inventory is not normally used or consumed, it is sold, so presumably for inventory, the deduction is allowed when the inventory is sold, which is the same basic way inventory had been deducted in the past, just under a different law using different terminology.

However, the new law included a second option, a HUGE change from the previous deduction rules. Inventory can be deducted using, to quote the IRS, "the method of accounting you use in your books and records that have been prepared in accordance with your accounting procedures." That bit of double-talk means that if you use the cash method of accounting, as most small businesses do, you have the option to deduct your inventory when you buy it. You may or may not want to select that option, as explained above, but it is available to you if you choose.

Curiously, the IRS has said nothing about this second, new deduct-when-purchased option other than the one sentence I quoted. The IRS provides no instructions how to take the deduction, where it goes on the tax form, or anything else. The IRS appears to be intentionally nonhelpful. But the law is the law, whether the IRS wants to talk about it or not. And the law has handed small business a major tax deduction option that never existed previously.

Thousands of people across the country have paid tax scheme promoters for the "secret" of not paying taxes or have bought "untax" packages. Then they find out that following the advice can result in civil and criminal penalties.

—Internal Revenue Service

Inventory Tax

Some local and state governments impose an inventory tax, sometimes called a floor tax, a property tax on business inventory. This tax is deductible.

Expense category: Taxes and Licenses.

Investment Credit

This is not one, but several tax credits lumped under one heading. Look up individual credits. Also see Tax Credits.

Expense category: Tax credits are taken on Form 1040, not on the business part of the tax return.

Investment Expenses

Money you invest in your own business may or may not be tax deductible, depending on what you spend the money on. Look up the actual expenses. Also see Startup Costs and, if your business is a corporation, Organizational Costs.

Investing (stocks, bonds): Investing, other than investing in your own business, may or may not be considered a business with allowable business deductions. See the discussion of investors in chapter 1. If your investing meets the criteria for being self-employed, most expenses, including broker fees, publications, and consultants, are deductible. Look up the individual deductions.

In a recent study, U.S. Treasury inspectors found that a large number of CPAs and tax attorneys who were surveyed failed to file returns, underreported income, or owed back taxes.

—Kiplinger Tax Letter

IRA

See Individual Retirement Arrangement.

Janitorial Service

Janitorial and cleaning services are deductible.
Expense category: Office Expenses.
Home-Based Business: Janitorial service is part of the Home Expenses deduction, not deducted separately. See Home Expenses.

Job Tax Credits

A Work Opportunity Tax Credit and an Empowerment Zone Tax Credit are available for employers who hire certain disadvantaged employees. Both of these credits expire after 2025. See Tax Credits.

Expense category: Tax credits are taken on Form 1040, not on the business part of the tax return.

Judgments

See Lawsuits.

Keogh Plan

A Keogh Plan, also known as an HR-10 Plan or a Qualified Plan, is a tax-deferred retirement plan. See Retirement Plans.

Expense category: Deducted on the 1040 form.

More information: IRS Publication 560, *Retirement Plans for Small Business.*

Kickbacks

Kickbacks that are legal and that meet the IRS's ordinary and necessary tests are deductible. Illegal kickbacks are not deductible.

Kickbacks often refer to illegal payoffs, bribes, and other wonderful stuff. But sometimes the term *kickback* refers, rather crudely, to rebates to customers or suppliers, or commissions or rewards paid for referrals. Some states outlaw some kinds of kickbacks. Illegal expenses are not deductible. If a payment is illegal in your state, it is not deductible on your state or federal return.

Expense category: Depends on how the money is actually spent.

Land

Land is not deductible until you sell it. Only the cost of a structure can be depreciated. For deducting or depreciating the cost of a building, you separate the cost of the building from the cost of the land.

Some land improvements, especially parking lots and major landscaping, can be depreciated. When purchasing land, separate out the depreciable items and any architect and engineering fees, which may be deductible. See Depreciation.

More information: IRS Publication 946, *How to Depreciate Property.*

Real estate developers: Predevelopment costs, such as planning and design, blueprints, building permits, engineering studies, landscape plans, and the like, are capitalized. They cannot be deducted currently. Some land developers may be eligible for the Domestic Production deduction.

Home-Based Business: Land improvements that benefit the entire house are part of the Home Expenses deduction, not deducted separately. See Home Expenses. Land improvements made only for the business, such as a customer parking or walking area, may be deductible in addition to the Home Expense deduction, though if you are audited, the IRS is likely to deny the deduction. If there is a significant amount of money at stake, I suggest talking to an experienced accountant who has home-business clients.

Landscaping

Landscaping, gardening, and lawn care expenses are deductible.

Expense category: Repairs and Maintenance.

Real estate developers: Landscape plans are capitalized. They cannot be deducted currently. See Depreciation.

Home-Based Business: If you take the flat-rate home business deduction (explained under Home Expenses), you can ignore this; it does not apply to you.

If you deduct actual expenses for the Home Expenses deduction (also explained under Home Expenses), the IRS prohibits deductions for most landscaping, lawn care, and gardening. According to the IRS, landscaping, gardening, and lawn care are not deductible for home-based businesses, even if done solely to enhance the image of the business. The only exception to this rule has been for home-based landscapers, if they are using the landscaping to demonstrate or advertise their services.

The Tax Courts have disagreed with the IRS on the landscaping deduction for home-based businesses and have allowed a tax deduction for landscaping, gardening, and lawn care costs if the business has clients visiting on a regular basis and if the appearance of the residence and the grounds would be of significance to the business operations. If the landscaping expenses are not significant, I suggest not deducting them. Why encourage an audit if there is little to be gained?

Just remember, the business belongs to you, not your accountant.

—Business columnist and CPA Gloria Gibbs Marullo

Late Charges

Late charges are deductible, except for government penalties. Penalties for late filing of government forms and tax returns are not deductible.
Expense category: Other Expenses.

Laundry Services

Laundry services for clothing used exclusively for work are deductible, but only if the clothing meets IRS requirements for deducting clothing. See Clothing. Laundry service for your regular clothing is deductible if you are traveling away from home overnight on business.
Expense category: For work clothes, Other Expenses; for travel, Travel.

Lawn Care

Lawn care, landscaping, and gardening expenses are deductible.
Expense category: Repairs and Maintenance.
Home-Based Business: The IRS says that lawn care is not deductible, but see the discussion under Landscaping. It also applies to lawn care.

Government is a reality of life. Denying it is just letting your own biases influence your business judgment.

—Bill McGowan, founder of MCI Communications

Lawsuits

The cost of a lawsuit is deductible in certain situations and not in others. The IRS has ruled differently at different times. Because of this, the information here should be used only as a guideline, as it may or may not apply in your own situation.

It appears from prior IRS rulings that you can deduct your legal expenses for a business or contractual dispute that does not go to court; for a lawsuit that goes to trial but is settled between the litigants before a trial is completed; or if you do go to court and win the lawsuit.

If you do go to court and lose a lawsuit, it appears that actual damages (compensatory damages) awarded to a plaintiff are deductible. Punitive damages (money you are required to pay as a punishment, not as a reimbursement or to cover a loss) are not deductible, at least not in prior rulings. Statutory damages (those specified by law or statute) may be deductible, but again, there have been conflicting rulings.

The IRS has also ruled that a settlement that Ides a nondisclosure agrelment is not deductible.

However, all these prior rulings may be moot. In a recent ruling, the IRS stated, "Liabilities incurred to settle a lawsuit, including legal fees and other expenses attributable to the lawsuit, are deductible as ordinary and necessary business expenses." This seems to contradict the prior rulings that disallowed deductions for punitive damages and judgments.

I do not have a definitive answer, but the wording of the new ruling sounds clear to me. I would take the deduction. I suggest you talk to an experienced accountant.

Expense category: For attorney fees, Legal and Professional Services. For damages, Other Expenses. If settling a business dispute, whatever the costs are actually for.

Lawyers

See Attorneys. Or maybe don't see attorneys.

I learned all the lawyer jokes from a friend who is a very successful and highly regarded attorney, who said a sense of humor is necessary to counterbalance the serious and often ridiculous legal issues lawyers face every day.

77% of small businesses polled think the existing tax system should be scrapped.

—National Small Business United

Leasehold Improvements

If you are paying for leasehold improvements on business property you rent or lease from a landlord (not property you own), you may be able to deduct them currently, or you can depreciate them over fifteen years. See Building Improvements.

Leasehold improvements include components of a building that are not structural, such as portable air-conditioning, some fixtures, support for heavy machinery, partitions, and awnings.

Expense category: Depreciation.

More information: IRS Publication 946, *How to Depreciate Property.*

Home-Based Business: Leasehold improvements are part of the Home Expenses deduction, not deducted separately. See Home Expenses.

Taxes have a negative impact on taxpayers.

—Martin Regalia, vice president, U.S. Chamber of Commerce, speaking before the House Committee on Small Business

Leases and Rent

Business leases and rentals for buildings, vehicles, and equipment are deductible, but with exceptions.

Lease-purchase: A lease-purchase, also called a conditional lease contract or rent-to-own, is considered a purchase, not a lease, and handled like any other purchase. A lease where you can purchase the equipment for a nominal fee at the end of the lease period is also considered a purchase. See Business Assets.

Automobile leases: There are limitations on automobile leases that are thirty days or longer. See Vehicles.

Leasing or renting equipment from employees: Payments to employees for use of their equipment, sometimes referred to as tool allowances, are a red-flag issue to the IRS, as the payments are often an attempt to disguise wages as something else. See Tool Allowances/Reimbursements.

Cancellation: A payment made to cancel a lease is deductible. A payment made to cancel a lease in order to get a more favorable lease is deducted over the term of the new lease.

Expense category: Rent or Lease.

Home-Based Business: A home lease or rental is part of the Home Expenses deduction, not deducted separately. See Home Expenses.

Legal Fees

Most legal fees, paralegal fees, filing fees, and related expenses are deductible.

Expense category: Legal and Professional Services.

Starting or buying a business: Legal fees associated with starting or buying a business cannot always be deducted the year paid. See Buying a Business, Startup Costs, and, if you are starting a corporation, Organizational Costs.

Also see Lawsuits.

Licenses

Business licenses and permits, and licenses for any business property, are deductible.

Vehicle licenses are deductible if you don't take the Standard Mileage Rate. See Vehicles.

Expense category: Taxes and Licenses.

Licensing Fees

Fees paid for the rights to use someone else's work, such as a trademark or an artist's photograph, are deductible, with some restrictions. See the listing for whatever it is you are licensing.

Expense category: Other Expenses.

Life Insurance

Self-employed individuals cannot deduct the cost of life insurance on themselves.

Employers: Premiums for group term life insurance paid by an employer on behalf of employees are deductible, but only if the employer is not a beneficiary. If coverage exceeds $50,000, the premiums are added to the employee's compensation as additional wages, subject to payroll taxes.

Expense category: Insurance.

Limousine Service

Deductible if it meets the IRS's ordinary and necessary tests for your type of business.

Be careful if this expenditure is considered an entertainment expense, which is not deductible.

Expense category: Other Expenses.

Lists

Fees paid to rent or acquire mail, email, telephone, or other lists are deductible.

Did you know that it is against federal law to make unsolicited telephone calls to people who signed up for the Do Not Call list? Last year the Federal Trade Commission received more than 300,000 complaints about unsolicited telephone calls.

Expense category: Advertising.

Customer lists: Amounts paid to acquire customer accounts are amortized over fifteen years.

Expense category: Other Expenses.

Livestock

Deductions for livestock vary depending on what kind of animals are being raised and what the animals are used for. Horses come under different rules than pigs. Dairy cattle come under different rules than meat cattle.

Generally, livestock that will be sold in the normal course of business, such as meat animals, is considered inventory. Animals that are producers, such as egg-laying hens, are considered business assets. This is a complicated area of tax law. I highly suggest getting help from an accountant who regularly works with farmers and ranchers.

More information: IRS Publication 225, *Farmer's Tax Guide.*

Loan Fees

Some loan fees are deductible. See Loans. Also see Interest.

Expense category: Interest.

Loans

A loan is not income when received and not an expense when paid. Repayment of a loan (principal) is not deductible.

Interest, loan fees, and closing costs may be deductible. See Interest. Points and other loan origination fees are deductible, but the deduction is spread out over the length of the loan.

Expense category: Interest.

Lobbying Expenses

You can deduct up to $2,000 to try to influence legislators or legislation, but only if the money is spent "in house," meaning you cannot hire an outside professional lobbyist.

Expense category: Legal and Professional Services.

Political contributions: Political contributions are not deductible. The IRS makes a distinction between lobbying (trying to influence a legislator or legislation) and political contributions (donations to candidates or political parties or political advertising). There is no $2,000 exception for political contributions.

Lodging

Lodging is deductible while you're traveling away from home overnight on business. See Travel.

Expense category: Travel.

More information: IRS Publication 463, *Travel, Gift, and Car Expenses.*

Employers: Lodging provided by an employer to employees is a tax-deductible expense if the lodging meets the IRS's ordinary and necessary tests. The cost of the lodging, however, is taxable to the employees as wages unless it meets three additional requirements: (1) the lodging is on the employer's business premises, (2) the lodging is for the employer's convenience, and (3) the lodging is required as a condition of employment. If these three requirements are met, the lodging is tax free for the employees. Owner-employees of S corporations are not eligible for this employer deduction for themselves.

Expense category: Employee Benefit Programs.

Corporations: Corporations can deduct actual lodging expenses or use a per diem rate. Noncorporate businesses cannot use the per diem. See Per Diem.

People make a mistake when they pay their legislators good salaries, expect them to work full time, and then complain about all the government intervention in their lives. The nature of legislators is to legislate. They work full time introducing new bills that create more agencies, bureaus, commissions and regulatory functions of government.

—Former California Senator H. R. Richardson

Logo

The cost of creating a company or product logo is deductible. Graphic designs and package designs are also deductible. However, if the cost is substantial (over $2,500), the logo has to be amortized over fifteen years.
  Expense category: Other expenses.

Long Term Care Insurance

Long term care insurance comes under the same eligibility rules as health insurance. See Health Insurance. Long term care insurance, however, is subject to a dollar limitation, which the IRS changes from year to year, and which varies depending on your age.
  Expense category: For self-employed, deducted on the first page of the 1040 return; for employers, Employee Benefit Programs.
  More information: For employers, IRS Publication 15-B, *Employer's Tax Guide to Fringe Benefits*. For dollar limits, IRS Publication 535, *Business Expenses*.

Losses

Some casualty and theft losses are deductible, some are not. See Casualty Losses.
  Business losses (showing a loss on your tax return) can be used to offset other income this year, and can also be used to offset profits from other years. See Net Operating Loss (NOL).
  Lost income: If a customer or client does not pay you for your work, there is no tax deduction for lost income. You simply don't report any income on your tax return. You have lost the value of your time and effort, but the value of time and effort is not deductible. If your loss includes goods and materials, you do get a deduction for the cost of the inventory, not the sales price you charged the customer. The deduction is part of the deduction for inventory. See Inventory.

Of course lower taxes are promised, but that has been promised by every president since Washington crossed the Delaware in a row boat. But taxes have gotten bigger, and their boats have gotten larger, until now the President crosses the Delaware in his private yacht.

—Will Rogers

Machinery

Machinery can be deducted the year purchased and first used in the business, or at your option, depreciated over seven years. For details and special situations, see Business Assets.

Expense category: Depreciation or Other Expenses, depending on several factors. See Business Assets.

Magazines

Books, magazines, newsletters, newspapers, and all other publications that are in any way related to your business are deductible.

Expense category: Office Expenses.

Mailbox Store Rentals

Mailbox store rents ("suites," as the mail order connoisseurs call them) are deductible.

Expense category: Office Expenses.

Mailing Lists

Mailing list rentals and purchases are deductible.

Expense category: Advertising.

Mailing Supplies and Expenses

Deductible.
> *Expense category:* Office Expenses.

Maintenance

Maintenance and minor repairs are deductible.
> *Expense category:* Repairs and Maintenance.
> Also see Repairs.
> **Home-Based Business:** Home maintenance is part of the Home Expenses deduction, not deducted separately. See Home Expenses.

Makeup

See Personal Appearance.

Management Fees

The fees charged by consultants you hire for management help are deductible.
> **Entertainers:** Managers (and booking agencies) who work for musicians and entertainers usually deduct their fees from whatever pay is coming to the performer. The income you get from the manager or agency has already been reduced, so you do not get to deduct the fee a second time. But if you pay any management or booking fees, or any other fees out of your pocket, the fees are deductible.
> *Expense category:* Commissions and Fees.

Manufactured Housing

See Mobile Home.

Manufacturing Overhead

See Overhead.

Manufacturing Supplies

Manufacturing supplies that go into the product being manufactured are part of your inventory. See Inventory.
   Expense category: Inventory.

Marketing

Most marketing expenses are deductible.
   Marketing is a broad term that includes advertising, promotion, news releases, catalogs, you name it. Look up each item that contributes to your marketing expenses to see if there are any limitations.
   Expense category: Depends on what is being deducted.

Market Research

Market research expenditures may be deductible currently, or they may have to be capitalized and deducted over a period of years, depending on their nature and the cost. Unless the expenditures are a large dollar amount (over $2,500), most businesses deduct them when incurred.
   Starting a business: Market research for a business you haven't yet started cannot be deducted until you are actually running the business. See Startup Costs. If you are starting a corporation, also see Organizational Costs.
   Expense category: Other Expenses.

Materials and Supplies

Materials and supplies are the same thing. See Supplies.

The best thing Congress can do is go home for a couple of years.

—Will Rogers

"Don't you dare deduct *me*."

Meals

Regular meals at work for yourself are generally not deductible.

But many meal expenses are deductible, or partly deductible, under a half-mile-long list of rules listed below.

Meals while traveling: Meals while traveling away from home on business are 50% deductible. Interstate truck drivers whose work hours are regulated by the U.S. Department of Transportation can deduct 80% of the cost of meals while on the road.

Meals with current or prospective customers are 50% deductible but only if business is specifically discussed at the meal and the cost is not "lavish or extravagant." The IRS requires that you have a receipt and write on it who you took out and why. Tips are considered part of the meal.

Expense category: For meals while traveling, Travel. If deducting meals with current or prospective customers, Other Expenses.

Also see Per Diem and Standard Meal Allowance.

Food samples available to the public are fully deductible. Food and beverages served at business-related events, such as a demonstration or exhibit, are deductible.

Expense category: Advertising.

Businesses selling meals (restaurants, caterers, food preparers): The cost of meals sold to your customers is 100% deductible. The food itself is considered inventory. See Inventory.

Child care and day care businesses: You can deduct the full cost of meals provided, not just 50%, or you can take the special Standard Meal Allowance. If your own child is one of the children, you are not allowed a deduction for the cost of food for your child. The IRS audit manual for child care businesses instructs auditors to investigate this flagrant violation of federal law.

Employers: Regular meals provided by an employer to employees are not deductible unless the meals are on the business premises and are "for the convenience of the employer." There must be a substantial business reason for providing the meals, such as requiring employees to be on call. If these requirements are met, the cost of employee meals is 50% deductible. Employers can deduct 50% of the cost of a company cafeteria if more than half of the meals eaten there were for the employer's convenience. This 50% deduction for employers will no longer be allowed starting in 2026.

Meals served to food service employees (restaurants, hotels, and the like) during or just before or after their shifts are 100% deductible to the employer and not taxable to the employees.

Snacks, bottled water, cold drinks, coffee, and doughnuts (or chai and gluten free not-doughnuts) are 50% deductible. Occasional meals provided to employees, such as a pizza party, the annual company picnic, or Thanksgiving turkeys you give your employees, are 100% deductible.

S corporations: If you are an owner-employee of your own S corporation, you are not eligible for the employee deductions for yourself. This rule does not apply to owner-employees of C corporations.

Expense category: Employee Benefit Programs.

More information: IRS Publication 15-B, *Employer's Guide to Fringe Benefits.*

Medical Expenses

Sole proprietors, partners in partnerships, member-owners of LLCs, and owners of S corporations are not allowed a deduction for medical expenses for themselves or their families. One exception to this rule is a medical expense or a drug test required by law for work, which most accountants say is fully deductible.

Medical insurance comes under a different set of rules. See Health Insurance.

Employers are allowed a full deduction for employees' medical expenses and for medical expenses of employees' spouses and dependents. Medical expenses refer to actual medical costs paid to doctors, hospitals, dentists, eye doctors, and other medical providers (including some alternative treatments) and for prescription drugs.

Spouse on the payroll: If you hire your spouse as an employee, you possibly may be able to deduct your medical expenses on your business tax return. Read "Spouse on payroll" under Health Insurance.

C corporations: If you or your spouse are an employee of your own C corporation (not S corporation), your and your family's medical expenses can be deducted as a corporation business expense, but only if you offer the same medical coverage to all your employees.

Expense category: Employee Benefit Programs.

More information: IRS Publication 15-B, *Employer's Guide to Fringe Benefits*.

Small businesses are very unhappy with the IRS. And I don't blame them.

—Former IRS Commissioner Charles O. Rossotti

Medical Insurance

Medical insurance is the same thing as health insurance. See Health Insurance.

Medicare Tax

The Medicare portion of the self-employment tax is considered health insurance, deductible along with any other health insurance premiums. See Health Insurance.

This Medicare deduction, however, has been disallowed in some prior years, the IRS going back and forth on their rulings. Best to verify the current IRS ruling before claiming the deduction.

Medicare premiums for business owners (that is, the insurance premiums you pay when you are on Medicare) are deductible under the same rules as health insurance. See Health Insurance. Note that Medicare tax and Medicare premiums are two different things.

Expense category: Taxes and Licenses.

Employers: All employees are subject to Medicare. Employers pay half the employees' Medicare tax, and the employees pay half. The employer's portion of the tax is deductible.

Expense category: Taxes and Licenses.

Meetings

Business meetings are deductible, although you are allowed only a 50% deduction for meals. See Travel.

Expense category: For the cost of attending a meeting, Other Expenses. For the travel and lodging, Travel.

Membership Fees

Membership fees for business associations and organizations are deductible, with some restrictions. See Associations. Membership fees to most clubs are not deductible. See Clubs.

Merchandise

Merchandise is another word for inventory, goods for sale. See Inventory.

Expense category: Inventory.

Merchant Associations

Dues and meetings are deductible.

Expense category: Other Expenses.

Political: If part of your merchant association dues is for political lobbying, that portion of the dues is not deductible.

Messenger Service

Messenger services are deductible. (This item is dedicated to the memory of John Cipollina.)

Expense category: Office Expenses.

Mileage Allowance
Mileage Rate

The IRS has a Standard Mileage Rate (Standard Mileage Allowance) for every business mile driven, for cars and some trucks. See Vehicles.

Miscellaneous

Although there are probably a hundred or more miscellaneous expenses a business can legitimately deduct, it is not a good idea to label anything "miscellaneous" on your tax return. The word *miscellaneous* is vague and can easily invite all kinds of questions from a suspicious auditor, especially if the dollar amounts are significant. It is better to use several smaller, more specific categories and individually list them on your tax return under Other Expenses.

Small businesses bear a disproportionate share of the burden imposed by all federal regulations, including tax regulations.

—U.S. Small Business Administration

Mobile Home

A deduction for a mobile home used for business depends on how it is categorized, whether it is considered a building or a trailer, and how it is licensed and taxed: as real property or personal property.

A mobile home can be either real property or personal property, depending on several factors. Real property refers to real estate, such as buildings and land. Personal property refers to all tangible property other than real estate.

If the mobile home is permanent, mounted on a foundation, and hooked up to utilities, it is usually considered real property. If the mobile home is in a temporary location, still on wheels, and easily movable, it is usually considered personal property.

An important consideration is how the mobile home is licensed and taxed by the state and county. If the mobile home is registered with the department of motor vehicles, licensed as a movable trailer, it is usually considered personal property. If the mobile home is on the county property tax rolls as a structure, it is usually considered real property.

A mobile home/trailer that is considered to be personal property (as opposed to real property) can usually be deducted the year of purchase. You also have the option to depreciate a trailer, write it off over five years instead of deducting the cost all at once. A mobile home that is real property is considered a building and depreciated over thirty-nine years.

Since personal property can give you a much bigger deduction this year than real property, it may at first appear beneficial to have your mobile home licensed by the department of motor vehicles and declared to be personal property. But most personal property is subject to sales tax, and most real property is exempt from sales tax. You may save a lot of money in sales tax if the mobile home is considered real property.

This is obviously a deduction that you want to discuss with an experienced accountant.

Expense category: Depreciation.

More information: IRS Publication 946, *How to Depreciate Property.*

Home-Based Business: A mobile home used as a home-based business is part of the Home Expenses deduction, not deducted separately. See Home Expenses.

The present system will not be abolished until all the members of Congress are forced to fill out their tax returns alone, without the help of an accountant.

—Columnist Nicholas von Hoffman

Mobile Phone

Mobile phones and smartphones come under the same rules as cell phones. See Cell Phones/Smartphones.

Mortgages

The mortgage payment on business property has several components, and each component has a different tax deduction rule: building, land, taxes, insurance, interest. Look up each item.

Home-Based Business: All the costs associated with a mortgage are part of the Home Expenses deduction, not deducted separately. See Home Expenses.

Motorcycles

The cost of a motorcycle used for business can be deducted the year purchased and first used in the business, or at your option, depreciated over five years. For details and special situations, see Business Assets.

Expense category: Depreciation or Other Expenses, depending on several factors. See Business Assets.

Part business, part personal: If the motorcycle is not used 100% for business, you prorate the expenses, business versus nonbusiness use.

The home based business is the last refuge from the bureaucratic meddling and stifling protectionism that inevitably accompany any and all government involvement. Those who long for government action on their behalf would do well to remember the axiom, For every government action, there is an overwhelming and destructive reaction.

—Home business owner Norman D. Wood

Moving Expenses

You may deduct all the expenses of moving your business from one location to another.

Expense category: Other expenses.

Home-Based Business: The business portion of the move is fully deductible, if you are allowed the Home Expenses deduction. See Home Expenses.

Multilevel Marketing

Multilevel marketing refers to a type of business, not to marketing expenses. If you are starting a multilevel marketing business, see Startup Costs. If you are setting up a corporation, also see Organizational Costs.

Musical Instruments and Equipment

If you are in business as a musician, band, or songwriter, the cost of your instruments and equipment can be deducted the year purchased and first used in the business, or at your option, depreciated over seven years. For details and special situations, see Business Assets.

If you buy a musical instrument to keep in your office just to use for your own enjoyment and relaxation, is it deductible? There are guitars in a lot of business offices, so I guess it meets the IRS's ordinary test. It helps you get through the business day, so I guess it meets the necessary test. And since it isn't a Prewar Martin D-28 originally owned by Hank Williams, it probably meets the not-lavish test. Me, I'd take the deduction.

Expense category: Depreciation or Other Expenses, depending on several factors. See Business Assets.

It's difficult to make your friends believe you make as much as you do and have the government believe you make as little as you do.

—Sam Leandro, professional musician

Music System

The office music system can be deducted the year purchased and first used in the business, or at your option, depreciated over five years. For details and special situations, see Business Assets.

Expense category: Depreciation or Other Expenses, depending on several factors. See Business Assets.

The cost of CDs, DVDs, music downloads, and music subscriptions are deductible.

Expense category: Office Expenses.

"You're saying that as a professional writer, your expenses totaled $22,000 more than your income? What kind of way is that to make a living?"

Net Operating Loss (NOL)

This is not really a tax deduction, but it can be a tax savings for businesses that have taxable losses.

If your business suffers a loss this year, you will owe no income taxes on the business, which I'm sure you know. You may not know that this loss will also offset other income, such as a·salary from an outside job or your spouse's wages or other taxable income, and reduce this year's income tax.

You can also use this year's loss to offset income and reduce taxes in future years. If the current year's income (if you have income from other sources) is not sufficient to absorb the entire loss, you may carry the balance forward to apply to as many as twenty future years.

Net operating loss is not simply the business loss shown on your tax return. It is a complicated combination of business and nonbusiness income and deductions. I don't include the NOL calculations because they are quite complex, and there's no way to simplify the procedure. They are explained in IRS Publication 536, *Net Operating Losses*. Don't be put off by their complexity. The NOL deduction may save you a bundle in income taxes.

Farmers: If you have an NOL, you can, at your option, carry the loss back two years and obtain a refund of prior years' taxes.

Expense category: Other Income; corporations use the Net Operating Loss deduction.

More information: IRS Publication 536, *Net Operating Losses.*

Networking

Networking usually refers to interacting with people to promote your business. Networking expenses are deductible, although you want to be careful that the expenses are not considered entertainment, which is not deductible.

Expense category: Advertising, unless there is an obvious other designation.

Network Marketing

Network marketing refers to a type of business, not to marketing expenses. If you are starting a network marketing business, see Startup Costs. If you are setting up a corporation, also see Organizational Costs.

New Businesses

Expenses incurred before starting your business and expenses associated with buying a business come under special rules. Tax deductions are limited. See Buying a Business, Startup Costs, and, if starting a corporation, Organizational Costs.

As soon as you start operating your business, these startup limitations no longer apply. It's always a good idea to postpone as many expenses as possible until you're actually earning income.

Newsletters
Newspapers

Books, magazines, newsletters, newspapers, and all other business-related publications are deductible.

Expense category: Office Expenses.

NOL

"NOL" stands for net operating loss. See Net Operating Loss.

Non-employees

See Independent Contractors.

Non-incidental Materials and Supplies

Materials and supplies (which are basically the same thing) that cost more than $2,500, what the IRS calls non-incidental materials and supplies, cannot be deducted until the year they are used.

Supplies that cost $2,500 or less, what the IRS calls incidental materials and supplies, are deducted when purchased. If you purchase supplies a little at a time, keeping each purchase under $2,500, you can ignore the non-incidental rules and deduct the supplies when you purchase them.

Expense category: For office supplies, Office Expenses. For other deductible supplies, Supplies.

Manufacturers and repair businesses: Supplies used in manufacturing or repairing a product are part of the cost of inventory. They are not deducted separately as supplies.

Inventory: One of the options for deducting inventory is to categorize it as non-incidental materials and supplies. See Inventory.

Notary Fees

Deductible.

Expense category: Legal and Professional Services.

Notes

Promissory notes and notes payable, like loan payments, are not deductible. The interest is deductible.

Expense category: Interest.

OASDI

OASDI (Old Age, Survivors, and Disability Insurance) for self-employed individuals is part of the self-employment tax and is not a deductible business expense. See Self-Employment Tax.

Employers: OASDI, also known as FICA, is the combined Medicare and Social Security payroll taxes deducted from every employee's paycheck and collected from every employer. The portion paid by the employer is deductible.

Expense category: Taxes and Licenses.

Occupational Licenses

Occupational licenses, fees, registrations, and the like are deductible.

Expense category: Taxes and Licenses.

Occupational training is deductible, with certain restrictions. See Education Expenses.

The National Commission on Restructuring the Internal Revenue Service, a joint House-Senate Congressional committee, after a year studying the IRS, recommended simplification of the tax laws as the key to a more "user friendly" IRS. Since the Commission's call for tax simplification was followed almost immediately by one of the most complex pieces of tax legislation in history, it was not clear how seriously its recommendations would be taken.

—Washington Post

Office

The cost of renting an office is deductible. The cost of an office building you own can be depreciated. See Buildings.

Expense category: If renting, Rent or Lease. If buying, Depreciation.

More information: For property you own, IRS Publication 946, *How to Depreciate Property*.

Home-Based Business: The cost of an office in your home comes under the Home Expenses rules. See Home Expenses.

Office Equipment

Office equipment can be deducted the year purchased and first used in the business, or at your option, depreciated over five years. For details and special situations, see Business Assets.

Expense category: Depreciation or Other Expenses, depending on several factors. See Business Assets.

Office equipment includes:

Adding machines	Credit card terminals	Postage meters
Answering machines	Desks	Printers
Cabinets	Fans	Racks
Calculators	Fax machines	Refrigerators
Carts	File cabinets	Rugs
Cash registers	Humidifiers	Scales
Chair mats	Lamps	Shelves
Chairs	Microwave	Tables
Clocks	Mirrors	Typewriters
Coatracks	Music systems	Vacuum cleaners
Coffeemakers	Pagers	Wastebaskets
Computers	Phones	Water dispensers
Copiers	Portable heaters	

Office Expenses

Most office expenses are deductible. See listings for individual items. Also see Office Equipment above and Office Supplies below.

Office in the Home

See Home Expenses.

Office Supplies

Office supplies are deductible.

Expense category: Office Expenses.

Office supplies is a catchall term. I tend to lump all kinds of low-cost business purchases in this category. It is a reasonably accurate description, and sure sounds better and less dubious than Miscellaneous or Other Expenses.

This is one deduction where inexpensive purchases can add up to a significant tax savings, if you keep track of everything you buy during the year.

Office supplies include:

Account books	First-aid kit	Pens
Bank checks	Flashlight	Periodicals
Batteries	Folders	Plant hangers
Beverages	Forms	Plants
Blades	Glue	Postage stamps
Books	Goldfish bowl	Post-it Notes
Bottled water	Greeting cards	Printer cartridges
Boxes	Headache remedies	Rubber bands
Brooms	Hole punchers	Rubber stamps
Business cards	Ink cartridges	Rulers
Calendars	Invoices	Safety glasses
Carpal tunnel wrist	Kleenex	Scissors
supports	Knives	Signs
CDs	Labels	Snacks
Cleaning supplies	Ledger paper	Small tools
Clipboards	Ledgers	Soap
Coffee	Letter openers	Stamp pads
Coffee	Light bulbs	Staple removers
Coffee	Magazines	Staplers
Computer disks	Maps	Staples
Directories	Moisteners	Stationery
Dust covers	Mops	Tape
Dustpans	Newsletters	Tape dispensers
Envelopes	Notebooks	Toner
Erasers	Notebooks	Towels
Fasteners	Organizers	Videos
File holders	Paper	Wite-Out
Fire extinguisher	Paper clips	
	Pencils	

Offshoring

See Foreign Expenses.

"Off the Books" Payments

Books is another term for ledgers, the financial records of business income and expenditures. Off-the-books refers to payments, in cash, that you intentionally chose not to record in your ledgers. Are they deductible?

Were the payments legal? If they were legal, they probably are deductible. If they were illegal, they are not deductible.

If you are paying an employee that is not on the payroll and should be, you are asking for serious trouble. See Under-the-Table Payments, which means the same thing.

Expense category: Varies depending on actual expenses.

On-Demand Workers

If you hire on-demand workers (gig workers, sharing economy workers), they are independent contractors. You deduct the expense as you would for any other contract work. See Independent Contractors.

If you are an on-demand worker, you are self-employed and eligible for every tax deduction in this book. Read "Gig Workers" in chapter 1. Also read Paying Yourself.

Operating Expenses

Operating expenses is a general term for the day-to-day costs of running a business. Look up the individual expenses to see what is and isn't deductible.

Operating Losses

Business losses (showing a loss on your tax return) can be used to offset other income this year, and can also be used to offset profits from other years. See Net Operating Loss.

Orchards

See Farming.

From the IRS's "Top Ten Filing Errors and Their Solutions for Small Businesses": Filing Error #1: Wrong name. Solution: Enter correct name.

Organizational Costs

This is a tax deduction that applies only to corporations. If you are not starting a corporation, this does not apply to you. Instead, see Startup Costs.

Corporations: Organizational costs are the legal and accounting services and government filing fees to set up a corporation (though not the cost of selling stock). Up to $5,000 of organizational costs can be deducted the first year the business opens, including costs incurred in previous years before the business was actually operating. Total deduction for organizational costs, current and previous years combined, is $5,000. Expenses in excess of the $5,000 maximum are amortized over fifteen years. The $5,000 deduction phases out, dollar for dollar, if organizational costs exceed $50,000.

The Organizational Cost deduction is optional. You can, if you prefer, amortize the costs over fifteen years. If your new corporation hasn't earned much money and will owe little or no taxes for the current year, by spreading out the organizational costs over fifteen years, you will save on future years' taxes.

Organizational costs end the day you start your business. All expenses after opening day come under regular tax deduction rules.

In addition to organizational costs, corporations (and all other businesses) can deduct startup costs for expenses paid before the business begins. See Startup Costs.

Organizations

Membership fees and dues for organizations, associations, and clubs may or may not be deductible, depending on the nature of the organization and what it spends its money on. See Associations. Also see Clubs.

Five million tax returns, Sacramento, California.

Other Expenses

There is an expense deduction item on the tax return called Other Expenses, a category that includes many different expenses. Some deductions are listed under Other Expenses because the IRS specifically says to list them there. Some deductions under Other Expenses simply don't fit any other category on the tax return. Look up individual deductions to see which expense category to use.

All the deductions you include in Other Expenses need to be individually listed on the tax return. The tax form has eight or nine lines to write in what you are including. If you have a lot of items, you may have to do some squeezing, or some judicious combining, or maybe pick a different expense category for some of the expenses. Keep in mind that the categories on the tax form are not carved in stone. The IRS is not going to deny a deduction because it is on the wrong line.

Expense category: Other Expenses.

Outside Contractors

Fees paid to outside contractors are deductible. See Independent Contractors.

Outside refers not to the great outdoors but to outside the business, that is, not an employee. The terms *outside contractor* and *independent contractor* are used interchangeably.

Expense category: Contract Labor.

Outstanding Checks

Outstanding checks are checks you have written that have not been deposited or cashed yet. The IRS says that you can deduct checks the year the checks were mailed or delivered.

If a check is lost, destroyed, or put on stop payment, if it is from the current year, reverse it out (make a minus entry) or delete the entry in your expenditure records. If the check is from the previous year, either increase the new year's income or decrease the new year's expenses by the amount of the check. No need to go back and change the prior year's records.

This agency intends to become an efficient consumer service organization, keeping taxpayers satisfied.

—IRS press release

Overhead

Most overhead is deductible but not as a lump sum. Look up each item that contributes to your overhead to see what is and isn't deductible.

Overhead is a broad term and usually refers to your "fixed" costs, the dozens of large and small expenses you pay whether you are generating income or not: rent, utilities, phone, insurance, office supplies, permits and licenses, payroll, and the cost and maintenance of tools and equipment and other business assets. These costs cannot be tied directly to a product or service.

Owner's Draw

Owner's draw—paying yourself—is not deductible.

The owner of an unincorporated business (sole proprietorship, partnership, or LLC) cannot get a tax-deductible salary or wage. See Draw. Also see Paying Yourself.

Package Design

See Design Costs.

Packaging Materials

Cartons, boxes, bottles, and other containers and packaging materials that hold the goods you sell are considered inventory. See Inventory.

If, however, the cost of the containers or packaging is not significant or containers are used only occasionally, most businesses write them off currently as shipping supplies.

Expense category: Supplies.

Never tell the IRS anything you don't have to.

—CPA Martin S. Kaplan

Pagers

The cost of a pager can be deducted the year purchased and first used in the business, or at your option, depreciated over five years. For details and special situations, see Business Assets.

Expense category: Depreciation or Other Expenses, depending on several factors. See Business Assets.

Painting

A minor or inexpensive paint job can be deducted currently.

Expense category: Repairs and Maintenance.

A major paint job, such as an entire building, can be deducted as a current expense or depreciated over a period of years. See Building Improvements.

Manufacturers and crafts businesses: The cost of painting inventory, including manufactured and crafted goods, is included as part of the cost of the goods. See Inventory.

Home-Based Business: Painting is part of the Home Expenses deduction, not deducted separately. See Home Expenses.

Paralegal Fees

Paralegal fees are deductible.

Expense category: Legal and Professional Fees.

Parents on Payroll

For children who hire their parents, the parents are considered regular employees subject to all regular employment and income taxes except Federal Unemployment Tax (FUTA). Parents are exempt from FUTA tax.

Expense category: Wages.

Corporations: The FUTA exemption does not apply to corporations. Family members employed by your corporation are treated like all other employees.

Parking

Parking at your regular place of work is not deductible. The IRS considers this a commuting expense. All other business parking costs are deductible.

If you take the Standard Mileage Rate, parking (other than parking at your regular place of work) is deductible in addition to the mileage rate. Parking tickets are not deductible.

Expense category: Car and Truck Expenses.

Employers: You can reimburse employees, and get a tax deduction, for the cost of parking near your business, up to $300 per month per employee.

The reimbursement is tax free for the employees. You, the owner of the business, cannot take the deduction for yourself (unless you are an owner-employee of a C corporation).

Whatever the revenue may be, there will always be the pressing need to spend it.

—Parkinson's Second Law, Prof. C. Northcote Parkinson

Parking Lots

You can deduct the costs of maintaining a parking lot or parking area on your business property. The cost of constructing a parking lot or area is depreciated. See Depreciation.

Expense category: For maintenance, Repairs and Maintenance. For construction, Depreciation.

More information: IRS Publication 946, *How to Depreciate Property.*

Home-Based Business: A parking lot, if you actually have one at your home, is part of the Home Expenses deduction, not deducted separately. See Home Expenses.

Parking Tickets

Fines for breaking the law are not deductible.

Parties

Business parties are considered entertainment and are not deductible. A sales meeting or a show, if it is primarily a business event, is 100% deductible.

Employers: A company party where all employees are invited is probably deductible. You should check with an accountant, as this deduction may be subject to disagreement.

Expense category: For holiday party, Office Expenses. For a sales meeting, Advertising.

Entertainment businesses: If you are in the business of throwing parties, these rules do not apply to you. The cost of entertainment provided to paying customers is 100% deductible.

Partners

Payment to partners in your business is not deductible. See Paying Yourself. Also see Guaranteed Payments to Partners.

A small business person has Uncle Sam as a partner, a partner who puts up no money, does no work, and wants 30 or 40 percent.

—Tax crusader Irwin Schiff

Parts

Parts that a manufacturer or a repair shop sells or uses are considered inventory, deducted the same as inventory. See Inventory. Parts, particularly inexpensive parts, that could be considered supplies instead of inventory (there is obviously some overlap) can be deducted as supplies. See Supplies.

Parts purchased to use in your business or to repair something (not to sell) can be deducted, under any expense category that seems appropriate.

Pass-Through Deduction

See Qualified Business Income Deduction.

Patents

Patent costs are amortized over fifteen years.
Expense category: Other Expenses.

Paying Yourself

Payments to yourself are not deductible, except for corporations.

If your business is a sole proprietorship, partnership, or LLC, you, the owner (or co-owner) are not an employee of your business. You cannot hire yourself as an employee. This is a point of law often misunderstood by new businesspeople. You cannot pay yourself a wage and deduct it as a business expense.

You may withdraw (that is, pay yourself) as much or as little money as you want, but this "draw" is not a wage, you do not pay payroll taxes on it, and you cannot claim a business deduction for it. The profit of your business, which is computed without regard to your draws, is your "wage" and is included on your personal income tax return.

Partnerships: Also see Guaranteed Payments to Partners.

Corporations: If your business is a corporation, you are an employee of your business. Your salary is a deductible expense of your business. See Wages. If your corporation is not making any money, or is losing money, you may not want to pay yourself a salary until the corporation is making a taxable profit. Otherwise you'll be paying payroll taxes and personal income taxes on the salary but getting no tax breaks for your corporation. This is an area of tax law you should discuss with an experienced accountant. There could be a lot of money at stake.

Expense category: Wages.

IRS Red Flag Audit Warning for corporations: Owners of corporations should be careful when paying themselves. The IRS often considers large payments to owners (large salaries, fees, or bonuses) to be disguised dividends, and not deductible as a business expense. This is not likely to be an issue with small corporations, as the dollar amounts are not usually significant (significant by IRS standards anyway). Still, it is something to discuss with a tax accountant.

Every April 15, I promise myself I'll be better prepared for next year's taxes. Then I turn to some more immediate concern, like earning a living, and forget all about taxes until next April 15, when I panic again.

—Tom Person, Laughing Bear Publishing, Houston, Texas

Payroll

See Wages.

Payroll Service

Hiring a payroll service to process your payroll is deductible.
Expense category: Legal and Professional Services.

Payroll Taxes

Payroll tax on self-employed individuals (the self-employment tax) is not deductible. See Self-Employment Tax.

Employers: Payroll taxes that an employer pays are deductible, including the employer's share of employee Social Security and Medicare taxes. Payroll taxes you withhold from employees' wages (the employee's portion of the taxes) are not deductible, because you are not paying those taxes, your employees are.

If this sounds confusing, keep in mind that payroll taxes have two components: the part paid by the employer, and the part paid by the employee that the employer deducts from the employee's paycheck. The employer sends the government both the employer portion and the employee portion, but only gets a deduction for the employer's portion.

Expense category: Taxes and Licenses.

More information: IRS Publication 15, *Employer's Tax Guide*.

Corporations: If your business is a corporation, you are an employee of your business like any other employee. You are not self-employed, and the nondeductible self-employment tax does not apply to you.

Penalties

Tax penalties and fines for violation of the law are not deductible. Costs of compliance and restitution are deductible. Penalties for not meeting contract requirements, and any other penalties or fines that do not involve breaking the law, are deductible.

Expense category: Other Expenses.

Pension Plans

Pension plans for your employees are deductible, but the rules vary depending on the plan you choose. You should discuss pension plans with an experienced accountant before making any decisions.

Expense category: Pensions and Profit-Sharing Plans.

More information: IRS Publication 560, *Retirement Plans for Small Business.*

Self-employed: If you are not an employer, there are several tax-deductible retirement plans you can choose. These are different than pension plans. See Retirement Plans.

Tax credits for employers: Employers may also be eligible for the Small Employer Pension Plan Startup Costs Credit. See Tax Credits.

Per Diem

For travel away from home overnight, some businesses can use a per diem rate instead of actual expenses. But, boy, the IRS really had a field day coming up with so many complicated rules, and for something that could have been so simple.

Per diem is French, or maybe Latin, for "by the day," a daily allowance. For people traveling away from home overnight on business, the IRS has established two per diem rates: a rate just for meals and tips, called Meals and Incidental Expenses, or M&IE, also known as the Standard Meal Allowance; and a rate that includes lodging along with meals and tips, called Lodging-Plus-M&IE. The IRS sets new per diem rates once a year.

Self-employed people can use the M&IE per diem. Self-employed people cannot use the Lodging-Plus-M&IE per diem. This per diem can only be used by corporations and by employers reimbursing employees. Self-employed people can deduct actual lodging expenses, just not the per diem.

Just to add to the confusion, you can only deduct 50% of the M&IE per diem rate, because meals are only 50% deductible. However, businesses using the Lodging-Plus-M&IE per diem can deduct the total amount of the per diem rate, even though it includes meals that are normally only 50% deductible.

You are not required to use per diem rates. You can take the per diem, if you are eligible, or the actual costs. If the per diem is higher, deduct the per diem. If actual costs are higher, deduct the costs. Nice deal, or to use another French (or maybe Latin) expression, *C'est la vie.* Also see Travel.

Expense category: Travel.

More information: For the current per diem rates, see IRS Publication 1542, *Per Diem Rates.*

The majority of errors on tax returns have nothing to do with the complexity of tax laws. They have more to do with carelessness or problems with the basics: reading, writing, arithmetic. You get to multiply, add, subtract and divide. It's not really difficult. And among the returns with simple errors were one million signed by tax practitioners.

—Tom Short, Director for Tax Policy,
U.S. Government Accounting Office

Periodicals

Business periodicals, magazines, newsletters, newspapers, and all other publications related to your business are deductible.

Expense category: Office Expenses.

Permits

Business permits and licenses are deductible. Some building permits may have to be added to the cost of the building and depreciated. See Depreciation.

Permits obtained before starting your business cannot be deducted until the business is actually in operation. See Startup Costs. If you are starting a corporation, also see Organizational Costs.

Expense category: Taxes and Licenses.

In this world, nothing is certain but death and taxes.

—Benjamin Franklin, 1789

The main difference between death and taxes is that taxes get worse every time Congress meets.

—Will Rogers

Death and taxes are certain, but death isn't an annual event.

—B. Bear, Pinball Alley, Willits, California

Personal Appearance
Personal Products

Generally, expenses incurred to enhance your personal appearance (makeup, hair care, skin care) are not deductible, even if the expenses are incurred solely to present a business image.

Businesses selling personal products: People who are in the business of selling personal products such as makeup can deduct the cost of using those products on themselves, because they are demonstrating or modeling the products. Tattoo artists may be able to deduct the cost of having themselves tattooed, using the same logic—you're sort of a walking billboard for your business—though that is not clear from any IRS rulings I can locate. If it was me, I would take the deduction.

This deduction does not extend to clothing. You cannot deduct the cost of clothing for yourself even if you are in the business of selling that clothing, unless the clothing is a costume or a uniform or clothing with your business name or logo on it. See Clothing.

Expense category: For the cost of the products themselves, Inventory. For paying someone to apply the products, Advertising.

Performers: Actors and others who are required to change their personal appearance for a specific job, such as needing a haircut to fit a role, have been able to deduct the expenses, but only because the change in appearance was required for a specific part and not the general appearance an actor wanted to create.

The IRS usually denies deductions for cosmetic surgery, though there have been exceptions for performers who would not be able to find work without changing their appearance. This is an area where you will benefit from talking to an accountant with experience in the entertainment industry.

Personal Property

Personal property—business assets other than real estate—can usually be deducted the year acquired or depreciated over several years. See Business Assets.

In tax law, personal property refers to tangible business assets other than real estate. Business machinery, equipment, vehicles, tools, and furniture are personal property. The word *personal* does not refer to nonbusiness.

Frivolous and false tax arguments say that paying taxes is voluntary. That's just plain wrong. The U.S. courts have continually rejected this.

—Internal Revenue Service

Personal Property Tax

Taxes on business assets are deductible.

Like Personal Property above, this tax is on business assets, not non-business assets. Personal property tax is levied on the value of business assets such as machinery and equipment and furniture, similar to the property tax on real estate. Some states and localities have a personal property tax, and some don't.

Personal property taxes can be quite high if your assets are assessed at a high value. You should examine the personal property tax bill, and make sure retired or sold assets are not included and that older assets are not overvalued.

Expense category: Taxes and Licenses.

Petty Cash

A petty cash fund itself is not deductible. It is just money some businesses keep on hand to pay small expenses. When you spend the money, you get a deduction for whatever you purchased.

If you do have a petty cash fund, be sure to keep a record of what you spent, so you'll remember to deduct it on your taxes. Expenses from petty cash are like the old fable of the baby calf the farmer's wife picked up every day. It wasn't much at first, but before she knew it, the calf had grown into a big animal. Those tiny expenses out of petty cash, and all the other dollar-here-dollar-there cash expenses, aren't much at first, but before you know it, they've grown into a big tax savings—if you remember to write them down.

Expense category: Whatever you spend the money on, once you spend it.

Photocopies

Deductible.
Expense category: Office Expenses.

Plantations

See Farming.

Plants

Office plants—the growing kind, not boilers and electricity-generating plants—and their upkeep are fully deductible.
Expense category: Office Expenses.
Plants—the industrial kind—are depreciated like buildings. See Buildings.
Expense category: Depreciation.
More information: IRS Publication 946, *How to Depreciate Property*.
Nurseries: Plants are considered inventory. See Inventory. Some plant production costs are currently deductible. There are specific IRS laws for businesses that grow plants. I suggest that you consult an accountant familiar with the nursery business, as there are special IRS rules for nurseries.

Points

Points are loan fees and cannot be deducted immediately. They are spread out over the length of the loan.
Expense category: Interest.

Political Contributions

Political campaign contributions, to a candidate or to a political party, are not deductible. Advertising in a political program or buying tickets to a political event are not deductible. So how do all these huge corporations funnel thousands of dollars into political campaigns to try to buy elections?
Also see Lobbying Expenses.

The IRS's primary task is to collect taxes under a voluntary compliance system.

—IRS Annual Report to Congress

Pollution Cleanup

See Contamination Cleanup.

Postage

Postage, post office box rents, and postal permits are deductible.
   Expense category: Office Expenses.

Post Office Box

Post office box rents and mailbox store rents are deductible.
   Expense category: Office Expenses.

Prepayments

Prepaid expenses that do not extend beyond twelve months can be deducted when paid, even though the expenses may be for part or all of next year.
   For example, you could pay for an insurance policy this year that ran from December of this year to December of next year and deduct the entire amount this year. You could pay for a policy this year that covered January through December of next year, and get the full deduction this year even though the entire period covered is next year, because the coverage is for no more than twelve months.
   Prepaid interest: One exception to this prepayment rule is prepaid interest, which is not deductible until the year the interest applies to.
   More than twelve months: Prepaid expenses that cover more than twelve months, and prepaid expenses that extend beyond December 31 of

next year (*not* this year), cannot be deducted until the year the expenses apply to. Only the current year's portion can be written off this year.

Expense category: Varies depending on actual expenses.

Deposits and down payments are handled differently. See Deposits.

Business assets such as furniture and equipment, purchased and paid for one year but not used until the following year, come under different rules. See Business Assets.

There is universal reluctance to voluntarily pay taxes.

—Society of California Accountants

Presentations

The costs of planning and giving business presentations are deductible. Travel and costs associated with travel are also deductible, though with limitations. See Travel.

Expense category: Office Expenses. For travel, Travel.

Prizes

Prizes and awards given to customers that generate sales or publicity for your business are deductible.

There is an important difference between prizes and gifts. The deduction for business gifts is limited to $25 per recipient per year. Prizes and awards do not have that limit. The distinction is whether it is "an incentive to generate sales" (a prize) or a thank-you after a sale (a gift limited to $25).

If you are giving prizes, how you deduct them depends on what you are giving. You deduct merchandise the same way you deduct inventory; see Inventory. If you are providing a free service, there is no tax deduction, because you cannot deduct the value of your own time.

Expense category: For merchandise given away, Inventory. For prizes that are not your regular merchandise, Other Expenses. For the cost of putting on a promotion (such as advertising and banners), Advertising.

Prizes are taxable to the recipient: Businesses that give prizes should be aware that prizes are taxable to the recipients, and that prizes valued at $600 or more have to be reported to the IRS.

Few people know that when they win a TV monitor giveaway at the local appliance store, they will owe income tax on the retail value of the prize. Or when a real estate agent gives a homebuyer a new washer or refrigerator as part of the sales deal, it's taxable to the recipients. And often, the winners are pretty angry when they find out. Especially, if they find out by getting an IRS 1099 form in the mail, which you, the merchant, are required to prepare for any prize that has a value of $600 or more.

If the prize is under $600, you do not have to file the 1099 form. You do not have to report anything to the IRS. The prize is taxable to the recipient no matter what the amount, but at least you don't have to do the dirty work of reporting it to the IRS.

Employers: For prizes given to employees, see Awards.

Product Development

Product development expenses are usually deductible. Development expenses that will benefit future years may have to be capitalized and amortized over five or more years. See Depreciation. If you have significant product development expenses, I suggest you talk to an experienced accountant.

Expense category: Other Expenses.

Tax credit: Product development expenses may be eligible for the Research Tax Credit. See Tax Credits.

Professional Associations and Organizations

Dues and meetings are deductible.

Expense category: Other Expenses.

Political: If part of your dues to a trade or professional association is for political lobbying, that portion of the dues is not deductible.

Travel: Travel to attend meetings is deductible, with some exceptions. See Travel.

You have reached the Internal Revenue Service. Due to the high volume of calls currently in our system, our representatives are unable to take your call.

—Recorded response, IRS help line, 800-TAX-1040

Professional Services

Professional, legal, and accounting services are deductible.

Expense category: Legal and Professional Services.

New businesses: Deductions for expenses incurred before you open your business are limited. See Startup Costs. If you are starting a corporation, also see Organizational Costs.

Profit-Sharing Plans

Self-employed people cannot set up profit-sharing plans for themselves, but they can have one or more retirement plans. See Retirement Plans.

Employers: Profit-sharing plans for employees are deductible.

Expense category: Pension and Profit-Sharing Plans.

Promissory Notes

Promissory notes are not deductible. A promissory note is a promise to pay money you owe, basically a loan agreement. The interest on a promissory note is deductible.

Expense category: Interest.

Promoter's Fees

Entertainers and musicians can deduct fees paid to promoters and booking agents.

Promoters, however, usually deduct their fees before paying entertainers. The income the entertainer reports on his or her tax return has been reduced by the amount of the fee the promoter deducted. No additional deduction can be taken.

Expense category: If paying fees, Commissions and Fees.

God bless our brave billionaires in these trying times.

—Professor and business writer Howard Karger,
University of Houston

Promotion

Promotional expenses are deductible. These may include brochures, audio and video productions, premiums, small gifts, greeting cards, or some service, performance, or show.

Sometimes there may be a fine line between what is promotion and what is entertainment. Promotion expenses are fully deductible. Entertainment is not deductible. The wise taxpayer carefully defines the expenses.

Sales promotions: How you write off the cost of sales promotions depends on what the promotion actually is. If you have a special sale, there really is nothing to deduct; you simply record the amount you receive as income. If you have something like a buy-one-get-one-free sale, again you record the amount you receive as income. The product you gave away is deducted as part of inventory. If you have a contest, the prize, if it is merchandise, is also deducted as inventory. Free samples are deducted as inventory. See Inventory for how to deduct merchandise. See Prizes for a warning about IRS rules for giveaways.

Expense category: For the cost of the promotion and small prizes, Advertising. For the cost of merchandise given away (other than small gifts), Inventory.

Property Taxes

Payments for property taxes are deductible.

In some cases you can choose to capitalize real estate property taxes instead of writing them off, adding the taxes to the cost of the real estate and depreciating them along with the real estate. If you choose to capitalize the property taxes (which in truth very few businesses do), I suggest you talk to an experienced accountant about the methods and options.

Personal property taxes: Some states and localities impose a property tax on business assets such as equipment, furniture, and tools. This is known as a personal property tax, although the property is not personal property but business property. The word *personal* refers to property that is not real estate. See Personal Property Tax.

Inventory taxes: Some states impose a property tax on inventory, called an inventory tax or a floor tax. This tax is deductible.

Expense category: Taxes and Licenses.

Real estate developers: If you purchase land that you plan to build on and sell, the property taxes are not currently deductible. The taxes are capitalized.

Home-Based Business: Property taxes are part of the Home Expenses deduction, not deducted separately. See Home Expenses.

Protective Gear

Cost of gear is deductible. Cost of cleaning is deductible.

Expense category: Supplies.

Publications

Books, magazines, newsletters, newspapers, and all other business-related publications are deductible.

Expense category: Office Expenses.

Punitive Damages

Punitive damages imposed by a government agency for breaking the law are not deductible. Any other punitive damages, such as for breach of contract, late charges, and the like, are deductible. See Lawsuits.

Expense category: Other Expenses.

Qualified Business Income Deduction (QBI)

You are allowed a deduction on your income tax return (through 2025) for up to 20% of your business or self-employment net income, but with exceptions and limitations covered below. This deduction is scheduled to expire after 2025.

This deduction does not require you to spend anything to get it. Unlike every other deduction in the book, the QBI deduction is not an expense you are writing off. All you have to do is have a business that is making a taxable profit.

Details:

Who can take the deduction: The deduction is available to all self-employed individuals and all types of businesses except C corporations: sole proprietorships, partnerships, joint ventures, LLCs, and S corporations. Farms qualify. C corporations are not eligible for the deduction. People categorized as statutory employees or nonstatutory employees (explained in chapter 1) can take the deduction. Rental income qualifies if you meet the requirements for being self-employed, explained in chapter 1. If you have more than one business, each business, as long as it is not a C corporation, is eligible for the deduction.

Deduction maximums: You can take the full 20% deduction if your total taxable income for the year, all types of income combined, is no more than $182,100 for single individuals or $364,200 for couples filing a joint tax return (before taking the 20% deduction). Note that the maximum for a joint return does not mean both spouses must be in business to get the maximum. If only one spouse owns the business, the business still can deduct up to the full joint-return maximum of $364,200.

If your income exceeds the above maximums, a different set of eligibility rules applies. Taxpayers with employees are eligible, and the calculations are based on the amount of your payroll. Read the rules in the IRS instructions for Form 8995 or get help from an experienced accountant.

Calculating the deduction: It is important to note that the business income you use to calculate the 20% deduction is not the net income you report on Schedule C. The 20% is based on what the IRS calls Qualified Business Income (QBI) and depends on several factors, including how much you pay in employee wages, the value of your business assets, and even what kind of business you operate. Tax deductions for health insurance and retirement and the 50% self-employment tax write-off all reduce your income in computing QBI. The formulas are complex and lengthy and will require help from an experienced accountant.

Expense category: Unlike other business deductions, the QBI Business Income deduction does not go on Schedule C (for sole proprietors), or on the partnership, S corporation, or LLC tax return. The deduction is calculated on a separate Form 8995 Qualified Business Income Deduction, or 8995-A Specified Service Trades or Businesses, depending on the type of business you own and the amount of income you report. The amount from 8995 or 8995-A is then entered on a line on your personal 1040 return. The deduction does not reduce your business profit, and therefore does not reduce your self-employment tax, but it does reduce your taxable income on your 1040 return.

More information: See *IRS Instructions for Form 8995.*

A final word about the QBI deduction: The IRS reports that many eligible businesses are not claiming the QBI deduction. Some businesses don't know about the deduction. Since it isn't an expense, there is nothing to alert a business owner that the deduction is available. Some businesses know about the deduction but are put off by the rules and the unfamiliar tax forms. These businesses have decided, I guess, that the tax savings aren't worth the time and effort it might take to wade through the instructions and calculations.

Qualified Plans

See Retirement Plans.

R&D (Research and Development)
R&E (Research and Experimentation)

Deductible. See Research.

Railroads

There is a tax credit for track maintenance. See Tax Credits.

Expense category: Tax credits are taken on Form 1040, not on the business part of the tax return.

Ranches

In the rural area where I live, the ranchers don't call themselves farmers, no sir. But the special tax deductions for ranches come under IRS rules for farming. That just ain't right, but the IRS tax writers don't live on ranches. Or farms. See Farming.

Raw Materials

Raw materials, a manufacturing term for the parts that go into whatever is being manufactured, is part of inventory. See Inventory.
   Expense category: Inventory.

An IRS audit of Summit Brewing Company in St. Paul, Minnesota, ruled that the monthly case of beer given to each employee was taxable income to the employees. The value of the free beer was $24.

—Reported by the *Minneapolis Star Tribune*

Razing a Building

The cost to demolish a building is added to the cost basis of the land. It cannot be deducted until you sell the land. See Land.

Real Estate

Most buildings must be depreciated, though some limited-use buildings can be deducted the year of purchase. See Buildings. Land cannot be written off until sold. See Land.
   Expense category: Depreciation (for buildings).
   More information: IRS Publication 946, *How to Depreciate Property*.

Real Estate Taxes

Deductible, but with limitations. See Property Taxes.

Home-Based Business: Property taxes are part of the Home Expenses deduction, not deducted separately. See Home Expenses.

Rebates

Rebates paid out are deductible. Rebates received are price reductions and reduce the cost of what you purchased. Also see Refunds.

Expense category: Depends on how the money is actually spent.

Postal Service, Civil Service, Selective Service, Internal Revenue Service. Confusing. Then one day I heard two farmers talking, and one said that he was having a bull service a few of his cows. Bingo! It all came into perspective. Now I understand what all of those "service" agencies are doing to me.

—Professor Iver Mindel, "At Your Service" Foremost Authority

Reconditioning

See Building Improvements.

Recordkeeping

Recordkeeping, bookkeeping, accounting, and similar services are deductible. Accounting and tax software that you lease or subscribe to can be deducted currently. Software that you purchase can be deducted currently or can be amortized over three years; see Software.

Expense category: For services, Legal and Professional Services. For internet subscriptions or access, Office Expenses. For software you purchase, Other Expenses.

Recreation Equipment
Recreation Facilities

Recreation equipment, if it meets the IRS ordinary and necessary tests, can be deducted the year purchased and first used in the business, or at your option, depreciated over seven years. For details and special situations, see Business Assets.

Expense category: Depreciation or Other Expenses, depending on several factors. See Business Assets.

Recreation and athletic facilities on the business premises that are open to all employees are deductible. Recreation facilities located away from the business premises may or may not be deductible. The IRS says there are restrictions. The Tax Courts disagree and say the facilities are deductible. If you own or lease such a facility, I suggest you talk to an experienced accountant.

Dues and memberships paid to recreational clubs are not deductible. Also see Vacation Facilities.

IRS Red Flag Audit Alert: To paraphrase those new age bumper stickers, Visualize Audit.

Recreational businesses: Businesses that are in the business of operating recreational facilities are exempt from these restrictions.

Once you become knowledgeable about the law, you can make the government agents go after the real criminals and leave law abiding people like yourself alone.

—Peyman Mottahedeh, Dean and sole Professor at
Freedom Law School, Tustin, California

Recreational Vehicles (RVs)

You can deduct the cost of using an RV for business, but with limitations. See Vehicles.

If you are using an RV for an office or business space (permanent, parked, not on the road), it no longer comes under vehicle rules. It can be deducted or depreciated like any other business asset. See Business Assets.

Mobile businesses and touring entertainers: If you are staying in an RV while traveling, your travel and living expenses are deductible (the cost of meals is 50% deductible). If, however, you are constantly traveling, living in your RV, the IRS considers the RV to be your home and will disallow most travel expenses, including the costs of operating the RV. This is a major issue with IRS auditors. See Travel.

Home-Based Business: A recreational vehicle used as a home-based business is part of the Home Expenses deduction, not deducted separately. See Home Expenses.

Recycling

Recycling pickup services are deductible.

Expense category: Utilities.

Home-Based Business: Recycling pickup is part of the Home Expenses deduction, not deducted separately. See Home Expenses.

Referrals

Commissions or fees paid for referrals are deductible.

Commissions paid to acquire new customers who sign long-term contracts may have to be amortized over the average number of years new customers stay with the business (however you determine that). If the amounts are minor, I would just write them off and not worry about it.

Expense category: If deducting, Commissions and Fees. If amortizing, Other Expenses.

Refresh Expenses

Refresh is a tax term for remodeling or renovating a building. See Building Improvements.

Refunds

Money you refund to a customer is deductible. On the tax return, sales refunds are shown in the income section as a reduction to income.

Expense category: Returns and Allowances.

Rehabilitation of Buildings

See Building Improvements. Also see Tax Credits for information about the Rehabilitation Tax Credit.

Reimbursements

Self-employed individuals who get reimbursed by clients for out-of-pocket expenses include the reimbursements as part of total income and deduct the expenses as regular business expenses.

Businesses reimbursing the business owners: If you are a partner in a partnership, an owner of a multi-owner LLC, or an owner of a corporation, your business can reimburse you for your out-of-pocket expenses, and the business gets the deduction. But the IRS requires you to have an "Accountable Reimbursement Plan," which is a written policy that the expenses are business related and substantiated: you have receipts. If you are a sole proprietor or the owner of a one-person LLC, you are exempt from this reimbursement rule. Any money you spend for your business is a business deduction, whether you spend it from your personal funds or from your business funds. There is no need to reimburse yourself.

Employers: When an employer reimburses an employee for out-of-pocket business expenses, the employer is entitled to a tax deduction for the expenses, but only if you have an Accountable Reimbursement Plan as explained above. If the employer's reimbursement exceeds the employee's actual expenses, the excess is considered wages and subject to payroll taxes.

IRS Red Flag Audit Warning: The IRS often considers employee reimbursements as wages in disguise, an attempt to avoid payroll taxes. Tool reimbursement plans, and what some employers call salary reduction programs, often lead to audits.

Expense category: Depends on how the money actually is spent.

Relocation Costs

Deductible, with limitations. See Moving Expenses.

**Remodeling
Renovations**

See Building Improvements.

Rent

Rent and leases for buildings, vehicles, and equipment are deductible, but with some exceptions. See Leases and Rent.
   Expense category: Rent or Lease.

Rental Businesses

Businesses that rent out any type of products—vehicles, equipment, furniture, party things like kiddie rides and bounce houses, or any other reusable goods—can deduct or depreciate the rental equipment just like other business assets. See Business Assets.

Repairs

Minor repairs to buildings, machinery, and equipment are deductible as a current expense. Generally, the IRS considers any repair that costs $2,500 or less to be minor, and deductible. For repairs to buildings, the maximum increases from $2,500 to $10,000 for buildings that cost $1 million or less.

Major repairs are deductible if they do not, to quote the IRS, "add to the value or appreciably prolong the useful life" of an asset. Whether a repair "adds to the value" or "prolongs the useful life" of an asset is, like beauty, in the eye of the beholder—or in the eye of the Tax Court, which has often overruled the IRS on the deductibility of repairs. Major repairs that are not deductible currently are depreciated over the remaining useful life of the building or the asset being repaired.

If you have significant repair expenses, you may want to talk to an experienced accountant about this deduction.

Vehicles: Vehicle repairs are deductible if you are not using the Standard Mileage Rate. See Vehicles.

Expense category: Repairs and Maintenance. If depreciating, Depreciation. For vehicle repairs, Car and Truck Expenses.

More information: If depreciating, IRS Publication 946, *How to Depreciate Property.*

IRS Red Flag Audit Warning: As I mention above, businesses deducting expensive repairs (in the thousands of dollars) have often been challenged by the IRS.

Home-Based Business: Home repairs are part of the Home Expenses deduction, not deducted separately. See Home Expenses.

Laws, they are spider webs for the rich and mighty, steel chains for the poor and weak, fishing nets in the hands of government.

—French printer Pierre Joseph Proudhon (1809–1865)

Research
Research and Development

Research, also known as research and development (R&D) or research and experimentation (R&E), is defined by the IRS as "developing, testing, refining or improving a product or service," a broad definition that can include many different expenses. Most research expenses can be deducted currently, or at your option, amortized over five years.

Expense category: Other Expenses.

Tax credit: Research and development expenditures, including some software development, are eligible for a Research Tax Credit. See Tax Credits. Market research is not eligible for the Research Tax Credit.

New businesses: Research expenditures cannot be deducted until the business is actually up and running. See Startup Costs.

We try to write at the lowest reading level that we can possibly write.

—Sheldon Schwartz, IRS National Director of
Tax Forms and Publications

Reserves

Reserves are funds set aside for some future use or an unplanned expense or loss. Nothing is actually spent, and no tax deduction is allowed.

Restoration

See Building Improvements.

Retirement Plans

The cost of retirement plans that self-employed individuals purchase for themselves are not business expenses, cannot be deducted on the business tax return, and do not reduce the taxable profit of the business.

Individuals who set up IRS-approved tax-deferred retirement plans can take a deduction on their 1040 return, which will reduce their taxable income by the same amount as if it was a business deduction. Income tax is the same no matter where the deduction is taken.

What *is* different is that business deductions reduce self-employment tax, which is approximately 15% of the business profit. Contributions to retirement plans do not reduce the self-employment tax.

Different plans: There are several tax-deferred retirement plans available to business owners and their employees. Each plan has different options, different contributions, different deadlines for making contributions, and, most important to employers, different requirements for including your employees in the plans. You can choose just one plan, or you may be able to set up multiple plans.

The different retirement plans include Individual Retirement Arrangement (IRA); Self Employed Pension Plan (SEP or SEP-IRA); Savings Incentive Match Plan for Employees (SIMPLE); Qualified Plan, also known as an HR-10 Plan or a Keogh Plan; Deferred Compensation Plan, more commonly called a 401(k) Plan; and Corporate Retirement Plan, also known as an ERISA (Employee Retirement Income Security Act) Plan.

You should talk to an experienced accountant, a bank or insurance company, or someone knowledgeable about retirement plans to learn the different options and the benefits and drawbacks of each. However, be cautious if the person giving you advice is trying to sell you a plan. Salespeople are not always unbiased.

Corporations: Some corporate plans have different deduction rules than plans for self-employed people.

Employers: If you have employees, some retirement plans require that any coverage for yourself also include your employees. Retirement contributions an employer makes on behalf of employees are deductible as a business expense.

Expense category: For employees, depending on the type of plan, Employee Benefit Programs, or Pensions and Profit-Sharing Plans.

More information: IRS Publication 590, *Individual Retirement Arrangements*; Publication 560, *Retirement Plans for Small Business*.

Also see Pension Plans.

Returned Checks

A polite term for bounced (bad) checks, returned checks are deductible as a bad debt expense. See Bounced Checks.

Expense category: Bad Debts.

Returned Goods

Refunds on returned goods are deducted from your income in figuring your taxes.

Expense category: Returns and Allowances.

Returnable goods: If you sell goods as returnable, you cannot take a deduction in anticipation of future returns. You may reduce your income after the goods are actually returned.

Rewards

Rewards to customers, vendors, and other non-employees are deductible, within limits. See Prizes.

Expense category: Other Expenses.

Employers: Rewards to employees, other than token nonmonetary gifts, are usually considered wages, taxable to the employee and subject to regular payroll taxes. However, employees can receive employee achievement awards that are not considered taxable wages. See Awards.

All taxes discourage something. Why not discourage bad things like pollution rather than good things like working?

—Former Secretary of the Treasury Lawrence Summers

Roads

You can deduct the costs of maintaining a private road or driveway on your business property. The cost of constructing a road is depreciated over fifteen years. See Depreciation.

Expense category: Repairs and Maintenance. For construction, Depreciation.

More information: IRS Publication 946, *How to Depreciate Property*.

Home-Based Business: A private road or driveway is part of the Home Expenses deduction, not deducted separately. See Home Expenses.

Robbery Losses

See Casualty Losses.

Many women tell me, "I'd rather pay more taxes than risk an audit." I never hear it from men. This is clearly a problem.

—Enrolled agent and tax advisor Jan Zobel, Oakland, California

---

Robots

The new hospital in the town where I live has a robot that roams the halls and visits patients. It has a video screen where its head should be, and it says it is a real doctor. Or whoever is on the screen says it's a real doctor. Or something like that.

Robots can be deducted the year purchased and first used in the business, or at your option, depreciated over seven years. For details and special situations, see Business Assets.

Expense category: Depreciation or Other Expenses, depending on several factors. See Business Assets.

Royalties

Royalties you pay are deductible.

Expense category: Other Expenses.

RV

See Recreational Vehicles.

Safe

A safe (the kind you lock stuff in) can be deducted the year purchased and first used in the business, or at your option, depreciated over seven years. For details and special situations, see Business Assets.

Expense category: Depreciation or Other Expenses, depending on several factors. See Business Assets.

Safe Deposit Box

Safe deposit boxes are deductible.
Expense category: Office Expenses.

I haven't paid taxes in years, one of the reasons I believe everyone should run a business.

—Shirley A., magazine publisher, New Jersey

People will do silly things to avoid taxes.

—J. C. Small, tax attorney, Counsel to the Director, New Jersey Division of Taxation

---

Safe Harbor

Just as a ship in the harbor is safe from winter storms, a business that stays within certain expense limits (meets the "safe harbor" requirements) is safe from the IRS's own version of winter storms: they won't audit you.

The IRS safe harbor rule, called the De Minimis Safe Harbor deduction, is for business assets but is also a guide to other deductions. It basically says (I am simplifying a long and complex law) that, generally, anything that costs $2,500 or less can usually be deducted the year of purchase and does not have to be depreciated.

Home-Based Business: Another safe harbor law, the Flat Rate Safe Harbor Home Business deduction, is a method for deducting home-based business expenses. See Home Expenses.

"MOST PEOPLE BRING THEIR ACCOUNTANT!"

Safety Equipment

Safety equipment, first-aid kits, fire extinguishers, and the like are deductible.
Expense category: Office expenses.

Self-employed individuals often cheat themselves by considering an expense personal when it's really a business expense. In the corporate world, it's clear who is a business associate and who is not. For the self-employed, that line is very wiggly. Just because someone is a friend or family member doesn't mean he or she isn't a business associate.

—*BusinessWeek* financial writer June Walker

Salaries

Any salary you pay to yourself is not deductible, unless your business is a corporation. See Paying Yourself.

Employers: Employee salaries are deductible. See Wages.
Expense category: Wages.

Sales Expenses

Most sales expenses are deductible. Look up the individual expenses, or pick an expense category that best seems to fit the expense.
Expense category: Office Expenses.
Also see Sales Reps.

Sales Refunds

Money you refund to a customer is deductible. On the tax return, sales refunds are shown in the income section as a reduction to income.
Expense category: Returns and Allowances.

Sales Reps

Deductions for paying sales reps (representatives) depend on how the reps are classified by the IRS. A sales rep might be an employee, might be an independent contractor, or might come under a pair of quasi-employment categories the IRS calls statutory employee or statutory non-employee.

How you classify and pay people who work for you is one of the most important areas of tax law. Penalties for misclassifying employees can be steep, and your liability if the person is injured on the job could be extensive. I highly encourage you to research the IRS requirements or get qualified help.

Four classifications:

Employee: If a sales rep is in fact an employee as defined by the IRS, the rep must be on your payroll like any other employee. How a sales rep is paid is not relevant. Even a commission-only rep might legally be an employee if the employment arrangement fits IRS guidelines for employees.

Independent contractor: Independent sales reps who meet IRS requirements for independent contractors are not employees. See Independent Contractor.

Statutory employee and statutory non-employee: Certain sales reps are considered statutory employees, or statutory non-employees, an IRS designation that allows certain salespeople to be treated as independent contractors. See "Statutory employees and statutory non-employees" in chapter 1.

Expense category: If an employee, Wages. If an outside contractor, Contract Labor. If a statutory employee, Wages. If a statutory non-employee, Contract Labor.

More information: IRS Publication 15, *Employer's Tax Guide.*

The IRS is trying to change its image. At the San Francisco Internal Revenue Service office, now renamed the IRS Customer Service Center, lobby signs now read "Please Wait Here" instead of "Wait Here." Agents wear colorful buttons that say, "We Work for You." The IRS no longer audits taxpayers, it "conducts examinations." The examinations are conducted by IRS auditors and they are the same as what used to be called audits, it's just that they aren't called audits anymore. As for quotas, they don't exist either. "We don't have quotas," IRS spokesman Larry Wright said. "The term we use is compliance statistics." Have a Nice Day.

—San Francisco Chronicle

Sales Returns

Money you refund to a customer is deductible. On the tax return, sales refunds are shown in the income section, as a reduction to income, rather than in the expense section.

Expense category: Returns and Allowances.

Business people often underestimate the number of able, conscientious and zealous people working for government in Washington— and Albany, Springfield, and Sacramento. They're usually overworked and underpaid. And motivated primarily by pride and faith in what they're doing. Try treating them that way. Walk in and say, "You're my government, help me." And they will, and love you for asking. It's a refreshing change for them.

—Robert Townsend in Up the Organization

Sales Tax

Sales tax paid on business assets should be added to the cost of the assets and deducted or depreciated as part of the cost of the asset. Sales tax paid on supplies and similar purchases should be added to the cost of the goods purchased. Do not deduct the sales tax separately.

Sales tax collected from your customers is usually included as part of your income and is deducted as a business expense.

Expense category: For sales tax collected from customers, Taxes and Licenses.

Gross receipts tax: Some states call their sales tax a gross receipts tax. But there is another type of tax called a gross receipts tax, different than sales tax. These are two different taxes. See Gross Receipts Tax.

Samples

Samples of your merchandise, given to prospective buyers or to people who might review or publicize your products, are deductible as part of inventory. See Inventory.

Expense category: Inventory.

Scholarships

Scholarships given to members of the community as a gesture of goodwill may be deductible as a promotional expense, especially if the scholarship is publicized. See Prizes.

Expense category: Advertising.

Employers: Scholarships given to employees are deductible, but might be taxable to the employees as wages. This is a tricky area of law—what is or isn't a taxable wage—that may require help from an experienced accountant.

SECA Tax

SECA (the Self Employment Contributions Act) refers to the self-employment tax. It is not deductible. See Self-Employment Tax.

Section 179 Deduction

This refers to the tax law that allows a business to deduct assets the year of purchase rather than depreciate them over several years. Also known as the First Year Write-Off. See Business Assets.

Expense category: Depreciation.

More information: IRS Publication 946, *How to Depreciate Property.*

Security

Security services and patrols are deductible.

Permanent and built-in security systems can be deducted currently or depreciated over a period of years. See Building Improvements.

Expense category: For services and inexpensive systems, Office Expenses. For permanent built-in systems, Depreciation.

More information: For built-in systems, IRS Publication 946, *How to Depreciate Property.*

Home-Based Business: An alarm or security system in your home is part of the Home Expenses deduction, not deducted separately. See Home Expenses.

Self-Employment Tax

Self-employment tax, also known as SECA (Self-Employment Contributions Act), is combined Social Security and Medicare tax for self-employed individuals. Sole proprietors, partners in partnerships, and owners of LLCs are subject to self-employment tax.

The Medicare portion of the self-employment tax can be deducted as health insurance. See Health Insurance, and also see Medicare for a warning about this deduction.

The self-employment tax itself cannot be deducted as a business expense, although there is a partial deduction on the 1040 form.

Expense category: Taken on Form 1040.

Corporations: Self-employment tax is not imposed on owners of small corporations, who are employees of the business and pay regular employee payroll taxes.

Telephone conversation between Irwin Schiff, tax crusader, and the IRS National Office:

Mr. Schiff: Is filing an income tax return based on voluntary compliance?

IRS: It is.

Mr. Schiff: In that case, I don't want to volunteer.

IRS: You have to volunteer.

Self-Insurance

Not deductible. Self-insurance is not really insurance at all, because no insurance policy is purchased.

Putting money aside in a separate account or reserve to self-insure for a possible emergency or loss is not deductible until you actually spend the money.

Seminars

Most business seminars are deductible. See Education.

Expense category: Other Expenses.

SEP
SEP-IRA

Contributions to retirement plans such as SEP are not deductible as business expenses. Contributions to a SEP (Simplified Employee Pension plan, also known as SEP-IRA) can be deducted on the 1040 tax return. See Retirement Plans.

Expense category: Deducted on the 1040 form, not on the business part of the tax return.

Employers: SEP contributions for your employees are deductible, within limits.

Corporations: Contributions for yourself as an owner-employee of your own corporation are a deductible business expense, within limits, but only if you include all eligible employees.

Expense category: Employee Benefit Programs.

More information: IRS Publication 560, *Retirement Plans for Small Business.*

Service Charges
Service Contracts

Service contracts and extended warranties are deductible. If the contract is for more than twelve months, see Prepayments. Weekly delivery service charges on a contract with UPS, FedEx, or other delivery service are deductible.

Expense category: Office Expenses.

Service Mark

A service mark is a trademark that applies to a service (trademarks apply to goods). Service marks are amortized over a fifteen-year period. See Depreciation.

Expense category: Other Expenses.

Settlements

See Lawsuits.

Sewer Service

Sewer charges are deductible. Sewer assessments, if for construction of new sewers, may have to be added to the cost of the building and depreciated as part of the building. See Depreciation.

Expense category: Utilities. For new construction, Depreciation.

Home-Based Business: Utilities are part of the Home Expenses deduction, not deducted separately. See Home Expenses.

Sharing Economy Workers

If you hire sharing economy workers (gig workers, on-demand workers), they are independent contractors, and you deduct the expense as you would for any other contract work. See Independent Contractors.

Expense category: Contract Labor.

If you are a sharing economy worker, you are self-employed and eligible for every tax deduction in this book. Read "Gig Workers" in chapter 1. Also see Paying Yourself.

It has become popular to call the Tax Code, "The IRS Code," suggesting that the IRS is responsible for it. The IRS didn't write it. Congress did. Congress is responsible for the tax mess, Republicans and Democrats alike.

—Kiplinger Tax Letter

Shipping

Shipping costs on goods you sell are deductible. Shipping costs for inventory you are buying are added to the cost of the inventory. See Inventory. Shipping costs for business assets you are buying (machinery, equipment, furniture) are added to the cost of the asset. See Business Assets.

Expense category: If deducting separately, Other Expenses.

Weekly delivery service charges on a contract with UPS, FedEx, or other delivery service are deductible.

Expense category: Office Expenses.

Shipping Supplies

Shipping supplies are deductible unless they are an integral part of the product you are shipping. If they are, the cost of the supplies is added to the cost of the inventory. See Inventory.

Expense category: If deductible, Supplies. If added to the cost of inventory, Cost of Goods Sold.

Shoplifting Losses

Shoplifting losses are not deductible. This is assuming you deducted the cost of your inventory, including the inventory that was stolen, when you purchased it. You do not get a second deduction. It's a lousy law, but it's the law just the same. See Inventory.

Showroom

The cost of renting a showroom is deductible. The cost of a building you own can be depreciated. See Buildings.

Expense category: If rented or leased, Rent or Lease. If owned, Depreciation.

More information: For buildings you own, IRS Publication 946, *How to Depreciate Property.*

Home-Based Business: The cost of a home-based showroom is part of the Home Expenses deduction, not deducted separately. See Home Expenses.

Shows

Shows you put on to promote your business are deductible. Food and beverages served are fully deductible.

Expense category: Advertising.

Shows you attend are deductible, though with limitations. See Travel.

Sick Pay

You cannot deduct your own sick pay, unless you are an employee of your own corporation. See Paying Yourself.

Employers: Employee sick pay is deductible. It is considered taxable wages.

Expense category: Wages.

Signs

Signs can be deducted the year purchased and first used in the business, or at your option, depreciated over seven years (fifteen years if large billboards). For details and special situations, see Business Assets.

Expense category: Depreciation or Other Expenses, depending on several factors. See Business Assets.

SIMPLE Plan

Contributions to retirement plans such as SIMPLE are not deductible as business expenses. Contributions can be deducted on the 1040 tax return. See Retirement Plans.

SIMPLE stands for Savings Incentive Match Plan for Employees, a tax-deferred retirement plan. And—I know you're going to be surprised—it's not all that simple.

Expense category: Deducted on the 1040 form, not on the business part of the tax return.

Employers: SIMPLE contributions for your employees are deductible, within limits.

Corporations: Contributions for yourself as an owner-employee of your own corporation are a deductible business expense, within limits, but only if you include all eligible employees.

Expense category: Employee Benefit Programs.

More information: IRS Publication 560, *Retirement Plans for Small Business*.

Simplified Employee Pension Plan

See SEP.

Skin Care

See Personal Appearance.

Smallwares for Restaurants and Bars

Glasses, plates, utensils, bar supplies, and the like are deductible.
  Expense category: Supplies.

Smartphones

Smartphones and mobile phones come under the same rules as cell phones. See Cell Phones/Smartphones. Business products and services that are ordered on a smartphone and billed by your cellular company are deductible.
  Expense category: Depends on what is being purchased.

Snacks

I looked this one up. Nowhere in the IRS Code does it mention snacks or say whether snacks are deductible. *Ooh, the peanuts are salty.* The IRS does allow a deduction for expenses that are ordinary and necessary. *Ah, the root beer is cold.* And everybody knows that snacks are ordinary and necessary. Absolutely. *We're out of chips. Do we get to deduct the mileage driving to the store to get more?*
  Expense category: Office Expenses.

Just be glad you aren't getting all the government you're paying for.

—Will Rogers

Social Security Tax

Social Security tax is part of the self-employment tax and is not a deductible business expense. See Self-Employment Tax.
  Employers: All employees are subject to Social Security tax. Employers pay half the employee Social Security tax, and the employees pay half. The employer's portion of the tax is deductible.
  Expense category: Taxes and Licenses.
  More information: IRS Publication 15, *Employer's Tax Guide.*

Software

There are many different tax rules for deducting the cost of software. Generally, most software can be deducted when purchased. If it didn't cost a fortune (under $2,500), just write it off and skip the next paragraph.

Software bundled with hardware (such as software that is preinstalled on a computer) is deducted as part of the cost of the hardware. Software you lease or subscribe to, such as cloud software, is deductible currently. Software you purchase (not custom designed for you) can be deducted currently, which most businesses do, or amortized over three years. If you purchase an app, the cost is deductible currently. A custom-designed software system specifically created for your business is amortized over fifteen years, although if the cost is not significant, most businesses deduct the cost currently. See Business Assets.

Expense category: Office Expenses. If amortizing, Other Expenses.

Software developers: If you develop software programs for yourself or for sale to others, you can either write off the development costs as current expenses or depreciate the costs over three years or five years. See Business Assets. Software you develop may be eligible for the Research Tax Credit. See Tax Credits.

The awful truth is that every software program is defective. There is no product out there that doesn't have bugs. Our favorite was a Tax Mate flaw that always printed the total tax owed as zero.

—PC World

We're not perfect.

—Gene Goldenberg, Kiplinger TaxCut software

Solar Power

If you purchase a solar electric system, you can deduct the cost or depreciate the system over five years. See Building Improvements for the rules.

Expense category: Depreciation.

More information: IRS Publication 946, *How to Depreciate Property.*

Home-Based Business: Solar electric systems are part of the Home Expenses deduction, not deducted separately. See Home Expenses.

Sponsorships

"Bob's Laundromat All Stars." Sponsor a Little League team, a race car, a rodeo rider, an event, or an individual in a show or competition and get a full deduction for your business.
    Expense category: Advertising.

It can probably be shown by facts and figures that there is no distinctly native American criminal class except Congress.

—Mark Twain

Sport Utility Vehicles

You can deduct the cost of using an SUV for business, but with limitations. See Vehicles.

Spouse

Some business deductions are allowed for expenses that benefit spouses, and some deductions prohibit expenses for spouses.
    For federal income tax laws, the IRS defines a spouse as anyone who is legally married. The IRS does not allow spousal deductions for couples who are not legally married. Different states have different definitions of legally married. Some states recognize common-law marriage, and some don't. If your state says you are legally married, the IRS accepts that ruling.
    Spouse's business expenses: In some states, both spouses are legally considered equal owners of all property and assets including businesses. Even though only one spouse may own the business, the other spouse can make business purchases and pay business bills and get the deduction for the business. A spouse cannot get a deduction for any travel unless he or she is a partner or employee of the business.

Expense category: Varies depending on actual expenses.

Spouse as employee: You can hire your spouse as an employee of your business and get a full payroll deduction like you would for any other employee. See Wages. Putting your spouse on the payroll will also make your spouse and family (including you) eligible for employee health insurance and medical expense coverage, all fully deductible. You will no longer be subject to the self-employment health insurance limitations. See Health Insurance and Medical Expenses.

Expense category: For pay, Wages. For health coverage, Employee Benefit Programs.

IRS Red Flag Audit Warning: The IRS believes (sometimes correctly) that some business owners put their spouse on the payroll as an employee solely to get the generous health insurance deduction. The IRS has often ruled in audits that the spouse is not doing real work, or is not doing enough work to justify the deduction. There is a big tax break if your spouse can qualify as a legitimate employee. I suggest you discuss this issue with an experienced tax accountant.

Standard Meal Allowance

You are allowed a 50% deduction for meals while traveling away from home overnight on business. You can keep track of actual meal expenses, or you can use the per diem Standard Meal Allowance. If you use per diem rates, the per diem rates for meals are only 50% deductible, because meals are only 50% deductible. Whatever per diem meal rate the IRS lists, you can deduct only half. See Per Diem.

Expense category: Meals.

More information: IRS Publication 1542, *Per Diem Rates.*

Child care and day care providers: You can use the Standard Meal Allowance or deduct the actual cost of meals. You can deduct 100% of the meals or 100% of the per diem. The 50% limitation does not apply to child care or day care businesses.

Special interest tax perks leave the IRS under terrific pressure to collect from ordinary Americans who don't have pals in Congress.

—Newsweek

Standard Mileage Allowance
Standard Mileage Rate

The IRS has a Standard Mileage Rate, also called the Standard Mileage Allowance, for cars and some trucks, which can be taken in lieu of deducting actual expenses. See Vehicles.

The IRS sends out more than 250,000 incorrect collection bills each year to individuals who have paid up.

—General Accounting Office, U.S. Congress

Startup Costs

Startup costs are actually pre-startup costs, those incurred before you start a business. Startup costs come under different tax rules than expenses incurred once you are open for business.

You can deduct up to $5,000 of startup costs. Expenses in excess of the $5,000 maximum are amortized over fifteen years. The $5,000 deduction phases out, dollar for dollar, if startup costs exceed $50,000.

You do not deduct startup costs before you start your business. You deduct startup costs the year you open your business, including costs incurred in previous years before the business was operating.

The $5,000 startup cost deduction is optional. You can, if you prefer, amortize the costs over fifteen years. If your new business hasn't earned much money and will owe little or no taxes for the current year, you will save on future years' taxes by spreading out the startup costs over fifteen years.

Startup costs end the day you start your business. Once you are open for business, all expenses come under regular tax deduction rules.

If you do incur startup expenses but never actually start a business, the expenses may be deductible as a capital loss under the IRS's capital gains and loss rules.

Expense category: Other Expenses.

Corporations: In addition to startup costs, corporations can deduct an additional $5,000 in organizational costs incurred before starting business.

Organizational costs are limited to legal and accounting services and government filing fees. See Organizational Costs.

IRS Red Flag Audit Warning: The IRS has often wrangled with taxpayers over which costs are and aren't startup costs and at what point a new venture is actually in business. I suggest you put off as many expenses as possible until the business is operating.

One way around some of the startup deduction limitations is to start your business at home, if that's feasible, just as small an operation as possible to meet IRS requirements. Once you have generated income, then spend your money on finding a new location, on furniture and equipment, and on accounting and legal advice. Since you are now officially in business, the expenses are deductible as regular business expenses, no longer subject to the startup rules.

Low-income taxpayers are being singled out for audits. I visited the homes of audit targets. Some were so poor they couldn't afford air conditioning in the sweltering Houston climate. What are we looking for with someone who does not have air conditioning?

—Houston IRS Agent Jennifer Long, testifying before the Senate

---

State Taxes

Most state taxes are deductible.

The list of state taxes on businesses is virtually endless. There is a tax on just about anything the states think they can get away with. If your state has a tax on something, you can be sure you will hear about it.

Special rules apply to sales tax and income tax.

Sales tax: Sales tax on purchases is added to the cost of whatever you are purchasing, not deducted separately. For sales tax you collect from your customers, see Sales Tax.

State income taxes: Only C corporations can deduct state income taxes on their federal returns. See Income Tax.

Expense category: Taxes and Licenses.

Stationery

Stationery, envelopes, and other office supplies can be deducted.
Expense category: Office Expenses.

Stock

If you are buying a corporation and acquiring corporate stock, as opposed to buying the assets of a corporation, you may be able to deduct some of the cost. This is a complicated area of tax law, and a lot of tax money may be at stake. You should definitely talk to an experienced accountant before buying a business. See Buying a Business.

The cost of issuing your own corporate stock may have to be amortized over a period of years. This is another area you should discuss with an experienced accountant.

Inventory: The term *stock* is also used to describe inventory, goods for sale. See Inventory.

Livestock: Livestock on farms may or may not be deductible, depending on many factors. See Livestock.

If it's in stock, we have it.

—Sign in farm supply store, Ukiah, California

Stolen Property

Deductible, but with limitations. See Casualty Losses.

Storage Costs
Storage Facilities

Storage costs are deductible. Rent of a storage facility is deductible. The cost of a storage facility that you purchase can be depreciated or, in some cases, deducted the year of purchase. See Buildings.

Expense category: For incidental costs, Other Expenses. For rent or lease, Rent or Lease. For purchase of a facility, Depreciation.

Home-Based Business: A storage space in the home is part of the Home Expenses deduction, not deducted separately. See Home Expenses.

Store

The cost of renting a store is deductible. The cost of a building you purchase can be depreciated. See Buildings. Also see Building Improvements.

Expense category: If rented or leased, Rent or Lease. If purchased, Depreciation.

More information: For buildings you own, IRS Publication 946, *How to Depreciate Property*.

Home-Based Business: A store in the home is part of the Home Expenses deduction, not deducted separately. See Home Expenses.

Store Fixtures

See Fixtures.

Storm Losses

Deductible, but with limitations. See Casualty Losses.

Expense category: Depends on kind of property lost, damaged, or destroyed.

Structures

See Buildings.

Studio

The cost of renting a studio is deductible. The cost of a building you own is depreciated. See Buildings.

Expense category: If rented or leased, Rent or Lease. If purchasing, Depreciation.

More information: For buildings you own, IRS Publication 946, *How to Depreciate Property*.

Home-Based Business: A studio in the home is part of the Home Expenses deduction, not deducted separately. See Home Expenses.

Subcontractors

Subcontractors may be self-employed independent contractors (contract labor) or may be employees.

Building contractors who hire subcontractors to work on their jobs can deduct the cost as contract labor if the subcontractor is self-employed. Building contractors, however, may have to put the subcontractor on the payroll as an employee, depending on the nature of the job.

Expense category: If the subcontractor is not an employee, Contract Labor. If the subcontractor is an employee, Wages.

IRS Red Flag Audit Warning: One of the IRS's biggest issues is employees misclassified as independent contractors (contract labor). This is an extremely important tax and liability issue for contractors. If you are unsure how to treat your subcontractor, I urge you to talk to an experienced accountant.

Subscriptions

Subscriptions are deductible.

Expense category: Office Expenses.

Supplies

Office supplies and miscellaneous business supplies are deductible.

Shipping supplies are deductible unless they are an integral part of the product you are shipping. If they are, the cost of the supplies is added to the cost of the inventory. See Inventory.

Manufacturing supplies are added to the cost of the goods being manufactured and included in inventory. See Inventory.

Expense category: For office supplies, Office Expenses. For other deductible supplies, Supplies. For supplies that are considered part of inventory, Inventory.

Non-incidental materials and supplies: The IRS distinguishes between supplies that are incidental (inexpensive and used up quickly) and non-incidental (lasting more than a year) and have different rules for deducting them. But few small businesses spent enough money on supplies (or materials: the same thing) to account for incidental versus non-incidental. All supplies can be deducted when purchased. The term *non-incidental materials or supplies* also refers to an option for deducting inventory, covered under Inventory.

Surveys

The cost of conducting surveys (getting people's opinions, not surveying property) is deductible. Surveying costs related to land or buildings may have to be capitalized. See Buildings. Also see Land.

Expense category: Legal and Professional Services.

SUVs (Sport Utility Vehicles)

You can deduct the cost of using an SUV for business, but with limitations. See Vehicles.

Tablets

Tablets such as iPads are deducted like computers. See Computers.

Tariffs

Tariffs, duties, and all fees and taxes related to importing and exporting can be deducted, although these expenses can sometimes be added to the cost of the inventory being purchased or sold. See Inventory. You may want to talk to an accountant with export and import experience.

Expense category: For tariffs and duties, Taxes and Licenses. For non-government fees, Legal and Professional Services. If adding to the cost of the inventory, Inventory.

Tattoos

See Personal Appearance.

The thing is a colossal mess.

— Former U.S. Treasury Secretary Paul O'Neill

Tax Credits

Tax credits are special tax incentives created by Congress to stimulate the economy, to encourage businesses to act in socially or environmentally responsible ways, or (I'm sure you'll be shocked) to slip a tax break to a favorite corporation or lobbyist.

Tax credits should not be confused with tax deductions. A tax deduction is an item of expense that reduces your business profit. A tax credit does not reduce your business profit. The credit reduces your taxes directly, dollar for dollar. For example, a tax deduction of $100 may save you $30 or $40 in taxes, depending on your tax bracket. A tax credit of $100 will save you a full $100 in taxes, regardless of your tax bracket. Tax credits are a real gold mine.

Some expenses can be taken as both tax deductions and tax credits. You get the deduction to reduce your taxable profit, and you get the tax credit to reduce your taxes! Tax credits come and go, available one year and not the next. Tax credits are taken on your 1040 return, not on your business schedule.

Small business tax credits:

Plug-in Electric Vehicle Credit.
Energy Credit. For solar and wind installations.
Foreign Income Tax Credit. For taxes paid to another country.

Research Credit. For increasing research, experimentation, and development expenses.

Low-Income Housing Credit. For construction of certain low-income housing.

Rehabilitation Credit. For rehabilitating a certified historic building.

Railroad Track Maintenance Credit.

Disabled Access Credit. For making your business more accessible to disabled people.

Credits for employers:

Family and Medical Leave Credit. Expires after 2025.

Health Insurance Credit.

Indian Employment Credit.

Pension Plan Startup Credit.

Child Care Facilities and Services Credit.

Work Opportunity Credit. For hiring disadvantaged employees. Expires after 2025.

Empowerment Zone Credit. For hiring employees in low-income areas. Expires after 2025.

Employer-Paid Taxes on Employee Tips (FICA Tax) Credit.

More information: A list of the most current credits can be found in IRS Publication 334, *Tax Guide for Small Business*.

Willie Foster, a minister and investigator for the NAACP in Fort Worth, Texas filled out IRS Form 3800 General Business Credit, requesting a $43,209 "Black Tax Credit." Mr. Foster stated, "It's about time they gave us something for that lost time in slavery." The IRS sent him the money. There is no such thing as a Black Tax Credit.

—Reported in the *Fort Worth Star-Telegram*

Taxes

Most taxes other than income tax and self-employment tax are deductible. See the listings of specific taxes for more details.

Expense category: Taxes and Licenses.

Sales tax: Sales tax you pay when you purchase goods is added to the cost of the goods, not deducted separately. See Sales Tax.

Tax Penalties

Tax penalties are not deductible. Interest charges on late tax payments are deductible for corporations only. See Interest.

Tax Return Preparation

Fees paid to prepare business tax returns are deductible.

For sole proprietors, only the cost of preparing the business part of your 1040 tax return (schedule C and related schedules) is deductible. Ask your accountant to give you a separate bill for the business part of the tax preparation fee, or just prorate the cost yourself. Unless you have a lot of nonbusiness tax issues, I'd figure that 90% of the cost is business related.

Tax software can be deducted currently. See Software.

Latest Revision For:

1040 Individual Income Tax Return

Department of the Treasury—Internal Revenue Service

Income Please attach Copy B of your Forms W-2 here.

Your social security number

1. How much money did you make last year? . . . . ▶

2. Send it in . . . . ▶

Expense category: For tax preparation, Legal and Professional Services. For software you lease or subscribe to, Office Expenses. For software you purchase, Depreciation.

Who does their own business taxes? Why would you do that? I don't even do my personal taxes, and they would probably take thirty seconds.

—Unidentified New Jersey advertising executive, *Inc.* magazine

I give all the papers to my tax accountant and just say, Here. I pay a lot of money for that privilege.

—Unidentified New York management consultant, *Inc.* magazine

---

Telephone

All business telephone services, fees, and taxes for landlines and cell phones are deductible.

Expense category: Office Expenses.

The cost of buying a telephone can be deducted the year purchased and first used in the business, or at your option, depreciated over five years. For details and special situations, see Business Assets.

Expense category: Depreciation or Other Expenses, depending on several factors. See Business Assets.

Home-Based Business: For home businesses, there are different tax deduction rules for landline phones than for cell phones and smartphones. If your phone is a landline phone, you may not deduct the basic monthly rate for the first landline into the home. You can deduct business-related long-distance calls, as long as you itemized them separately, but not the basic monthly rate. Any additional landlines into the house after the first telephone line, if used exclusively for business, are fully deductible. Cell phones and smartphones do not have this restriction.

Laws are like sausages, it is better not to see them being made.

—Chancellor Otto von Bismarck (1815–1898)

Temporary Help Agency

Fees paid to an agency or service that provides temporary workers are fully deductible. The workers are not your employees, they are employees of the agency, so this is not a payroll expense.

Be careful when contracting with a temporary help agency that the workers are in fact employed by the agency, and not able to be considered your employees. Don't pay the workers directly or any of the workers' payroll taxes or health insurance. Examine the contract with the agency to be sure you are not liable for any employer responsibilities.

Expense category: Legal and Professional Services.

1099 Workers

This is a term some people use to describe gig workers, who are actually independent contractors. See Independent Contractors.

Thank-You Cards

Deductible, and encouraged. Little details like thank-you cards bring customers back.

Expense category: Office Expenses.

Theft Losses

See Casualty Losses.

This Book

That's right. The money you paid for this book is 100% deductible. In fact, you can deduct twice as much just by going out and buying a second copy.

Expense category: Office Expenses.

Tickets

Tickets to events such as sports, music, and theater are considered entertainment and are not deductible. If, however, you buy tickets to give as business gifts, you can deduct up to $25 per gift. See Business Gifts.

Raffle tickets are usually not deductible. Parking tickets, speeding tickets, and other citations for illegal activities are not deductible.

I'm not his father, and he doesn't need a nursemaid. I just tell him, don't forget to pay your taxes. I tell him that every week when he's working. I've seen too many people get into bad trouble by forgetting to pay their taxes.

—Elvis Presley's longtime manager, Col. Tom Parker, 1960

Tips

Tip #1: Don't open any email attachments from Nigeria.

Tip #2: Don't tell the IRS auditor that income taxes are unconstitutional.

Tip #3: Tips paid for meal service are 50% deductible if you are traveling away from home overnight. Tips for services other than food are fully deductible.

Expense category: Meals. Other Expenses.

Restaurant and tavern employers: There is a tax credit for payroll taxes paid on employee tips. See Tax Credits.

Tolls

Vehicle tolls are deductible. If you take the Standard Mileage Rate, tolls are deductible in addition to the mileage allowance. See Vehicles.

Expense category: Car and Truck Expenses.

What the mindless politicians and the equally mindless media don't take into account is that the country is run by the great financial powers and corporate interests, and they send their lawyers to Congress to make laws so that they don't have to pay taxes.

—Writer Gore Vidal

Tool Allowances/Reimbursements

Payments to employees for use of their tools or equipment are considered taxable wages, unless the payments are part of a formal "Accountable Reimbursement Plan," a written policy that the expenses are business related and that they are substantiated (you have receipts).

IRS Red Flag Audit Warning: Tool allowances and similar arrangements that attempt to avoid paying wages, and to avoid payroll taxes, invite audits. Even with an Accountable Reimbursement Plan, the IRS is likely to challenge the deduction. This is definitely a hot-button issue with the IRS.

Tools

Tools can be deducted the year purchased and first used in the business, or at your option, depreciated over seven years. For details and special situations, see Business Assets.

Expense category: Depreciation or Other Expenses, depending on several factors. See Business Assets.

Tour Bus

See Bus.

Touring Expenses

See Travel.

Tractors

Tractors and construction equipment can be deducted the year purchased and first used in the business, or at your option, depreciated over seven years. For details and special situations, see Business Assets.

Expense category: Depreciation or Other Expenses, depending on several factors. See Business Assets.

The American War of Independence had its origin in the refusal to pay taxes imposed by Britain. Constitutional scholars argue to this day whether the framers of the Constitution ruled out or allowed an income tax. But for 85 years, no income tax was ever considered, until the government ran short of funds during the Civil War. The Act of Congress of August 5, 1861 imposed a 3% federal income tax. The Supreme Court ruled it unconstitutional. Congress, determined to have an income tax, voted 318 to 14 for the Sixteenth Amendment in 1909.

—The Law and the Profits, by Professor C. Northcote Parkinson

---

Trade

Trade, as in exchange or barter, is a taxable transaction. See Barter/Trade.
Expense category: Depends on what is acquired in trade.

Trade Association

Dues and meetings are deductible.
Expense category: Other Expenses.
Political: If part of your dues to a trade or professional association are for political lobbying, that portion of the dues is not deductible.

Trade Dress

Trade dress is a form of trademark. The cost is amortized over a fifteen-year period.
Expense category: Other Expenses.

Trademark

The cost of obtaining a trademark—or a service mark, trade name, or trade dress—is amortized over a fifteen-year period. See Depreciation. Licensed trademarks can be deducted currently if you will not be using the license for more than a year.

Domain names that are trademarked are also amortized over fifteen years.

Expense category: Other Expenses.

Trade Name

Trade names are similar to trademarks. The cost is amortized over a fifteen-year period.

Expense category: Other Expenses.

What's bad news for some is a bonanza for others. Those tens of billions in costs are going into the pockets of tens of thousands of tax preparers who are organized and love complexity as much as the rest of us hate it.

—Columnist Nicholas von Hoffman

From a tax lawyer's point of view, we're in heaven.

—Tax attorney Leslie B. Samuels

Trade Show

Admission fees to trade shows are deductible. Travel and lodging are deductible. Meals are 50% deductible. See Travel.

Expense category: For admission, Other Expenses. For travel, Travel.

Trailers

Travel trailers, utility trailers, and movable mobile homes can be deducted the year purchased and first used in the business, or at your option, depreciated over five years. For details and special situations, see Business Assets.

Expense category: Depreciation or Other Expenses, depending on several factors. See Business Assets.

Mobile homes that are permanent (on foundations) are usually considered real property and are depreciated. See Mobile Home.

Mobile businesses and touring entertainers: If you are staying in a trailer while traveling, your travel and living expenses are deductible (the cost of meals is 50% deductible). If, however, you are constantly traveling, living in your trailer, the IRS considers the trailer to be your home and will disallow travel expenses. This is a major issue with IRS auditors. See Travel.

Home-Based Business: A trailer used as a business space on your home property is part of the Home Expenses deduction, not deducted separately. See Home Expenses.

Training

Training expenses, seminars, videos, and manuals are deductible, but with limitations. See Education Expenses.

Expense category: Other Expenses.

Americans love taxes that other people pay.

—Columnist Debra J. Saunders

Transit Passes

See Commuting.

Transportation

Local transportation expenses are deductible except commuting expenses, home to your regular place of work and back, which are not deductible. See Commuting.

Expense category: For a vehicle you own, rent, or lease, see Vehicles. For other local transportation, Office Expenses. Do not put local transportation expenses under Travel, which is for overnight travel.

Also see Vehicles.

Travel

This deduction, and the lengthy IRS rules for travel, apply only to overnight travel. For local transportation, see Transportation and Commuting.

Self-employed individuals are allowed a 50% deduction for meals and a full 100% deduction for lodging and miscellaneous expenses if you are away from home overnight on business.

The definition of home is important here. According to the IRS, "home" is your place of business, not where you live. People who work far from home and stay overnight near work cannot deduct the cost. Self-employed

Write off your horse. Work your horse into your act and deduct all its touring costs, including the truck and trailer, boarding, feed, veterinary fees, horseshoeing, and the saddle. You can even depreciate the horse. Back in the saddle again.

itinerant workers, traveling contractors, and salespeople who are continually on the road are often denied travel deductions, the IRS claiming that the road is home, so nothing is allowed. This has been an issue of contention for years, one that the IRS sometimes wins and sometimes doesn't. If you make your living on the road, I suggest you talk to an experienced accountant. If you are working away from home for over one year, the IRS automatically considers the road to be home and disallows travel expenses.

If you are eligible for travel deductions, there are a lot of rules. Not everything is deductible. The rules vary depending on where you are going, why you're going, how you get there, how long you're staying, and how much of the trip is for business versus nonbusiness.

100% business: A business trip that is entirely for business, in or outside the United States, is deductible. Round-trip travel, lodging, transportation, and incidental expenses are 100% deductible. Meals are 50% deductible. Tax deductions for travel on cruise ships, unless the cruise is a seminar or convention or business meeting, is subject to maximum daily limits.

There are restrictions on overseas travel to attend a convention, seminar, or meeting outside North America. If it is "reasonable" (to quote the IRS) to hold the meeting in that country, the deduction is allowed. The IRS has provided no guidelines as to what they mean by "reasonable," so I guess you get to make your own. An opportunity like that sounds reasonable to me.

Business and vacation combined: For a trip that is part business and part vacation, you may be able to deduct some of it, and you may be able to deduct all of it.

If the reason for your trip is primarily personal (more than half the days are for vacation), none of the traveling expenses to and from your destination are deductible. Only expenses directly related to your business can be deducted.

If your trip is primarily for business (more than half the days are for business) and it is within the United States, the cost of the round trip travel is fully deductible, even if some of the trip is for pleasure. So you can tack a short vacation onto a business trip, and the only costs that aren't deductible are the nonbusiness expenses, such as the extra days' lodging and meals.

When counting business versus vacation days, a business day does not require you to do business all day. Any day you put in at least four hours of work is considered a business day. Any day your presence is required, for any amount of time, is considered a business day. And travel days also count as business days.

If you have a business trip that overlaps a weekend, requiring you to be there Friday and the following Monday, lucky you. You can write off the weekend as a business expense as well, even though all you did was sit on the beach and dance in the clubs (as long as it is less expensive to stay the weekend than to go home Friday and come back Monday morning).

If you travel outside the United States, more stringent rules apply. If the trip is no more than one week or the time spent for pleasure is less than 25%, the same basic rules apply as a trip within the United States. But if the trip is more than a week, or if the vacation days are 25% or more of the trip, you allocate travel expenses between the business and personal portions of your trip.

Deductible travel expenses: Cost of transportation to and from your destination. Lodging and 50% of the cost of meals. Cost of transportation while away from home such as local rides and auto rentals. Incidental and personal services such as laundry and hair care. For meals and lodging, you can keep a record of actual expenses, or for some businesses, you can use a standard per diem rate set by the IRS: so much per day. See Per Diem and Standard Meal Allowance.

Spouse, family, friend: Travel expenses are not deductible for your spouse, dependent, friend, or anyone else unless he or she is an employee or co-owner of the business and there is a bona fide business purpose for accompanying you.

Expense category: Travel.

More information: IRS Publication 463, *Travel, Gift, and Car Expenses*; IRS Publication 1542, *Per Diem Rates*.

Travel agents: Travel agents often claim they need to travel in order to be able to better advise their clients, that such travel expenses are ordinary and necessary expenses of their business and are therefore fully deductible. The IRS does not always agree, especially if the travel expenses are significant compared to the income generated from the business. In audits, the IRS sometimes allows travel deductions and sometimes disallows the deductions.

Employers can reimburse employees for travel expenses and get a deduction, but be careful to follow the rules. See Reimbursements.

IRS Red Flag Audit Warning: The IRS does not like business trips. As you can tell from the generous way the law is written, it's a bit too easy to write off a business trip that is really a disguised vacation. The IRS knows this, and they are forever suspicious of business travel expenses, particularly for sole proprietorships where the owner is accountable to no one else: you feel like taking a business trip (and you can afford it), you take it. The IRS wants to be sure it's not a vacation in disguise. You want to be sure you can prove, if audited, that the trip wasn't a vacation. A log of daily activities and business contacts is not required by law, but it may help convince a skeptical IRS auditor that your trip to the Bahamas really was for business. Take photographs of businesses you visited or goods you want to carry.

The hired help in Washington have been busy beavers this year. . . . There's so much they have to do and yet they still have time to think of new ways to dip even deeper into our pockets.

—Businessman Roger Ott

Trips (Business)

For overnight business trips, see Travel. For local travel, see Transportation.

Trucks

You can deduct the cost of using a truck for business. Different types of trucks, however, come under different rules. See Vehicles.

Tuition

Some tuition is deductible. See Education Expenses.

Typewriter

Yes, you can still buy a typewriter and you can still get one fixed. There are 250 typewriter sales and repair shops in the United States and one remaining manufacturer.

Typewriters can be deducted the year purchased and first used in the business, or at your option, depreciated over five years. For details and special situations, see Business Assets.

Expense category: Depreciation or Other Expenses, depending on several factors. See Business Assets.

Uncashed Checks

A check mailed or delivered by December 31 can be deducted the year it was written even though it was not cashed until the new year.

If a check never gets cashed—if it is lost, destroyed, or put on stop payment—and if it is from the current year, reverse it out (make a minus entry) or delete the entry in your expenditure records. If the check is from the previous year, either increase the new year's income or decrease the new year's expenses by the amount of the check. No need to go back and change the prior year's records.

Uncollectible Accounts

Businesses using the cash method of accounting—the method used by most small businesses, recording income when the money comes in—cannot take a deduction for uncollectible accounts, because the lost income was never recorded.

This is probably the one deduction (nondeduction) that hurts the most. You did the work, put in the time, you don't get paid, and you can't even write it off.

If the unpaid sale was for merchandise, you do get a deduction for cost of the inventory, if you haven't already deducted the inventory when you purchased it. See Inventory.

But you don't get a deduction for the time you put in. This is explained under Paying Yourself.

Businesses using accrual accounting: Under accrual accounting, income is recorded when you make a sale, whether or not you were paid at the time of the sale. Accrual businesses can take a bad debt expense for an uncollectible account, equal to the income you recorded but never received. Few if any small businesses use accrual accounting because it is much more complicated than cash basis accounting. You can learn more about this in chapter 1.

Under-the-Table Payments

Is an under-the-table payment deductible? If the payment was illegal, no deduction is allowed. If it was legal, it is deductible, depending on what the payment was for.

Under the table means that a payment has been made, secretly, in cash, and no record is made of the payment. Under-the-table payments are sometimes made (so I'm told) to workers who are not officially on the payroll to avoid payroll taxes and workers' compensation insurance premiums, which is illegal and very risky and not a good idea at all.

If the under-the-table payment was legal, it is deductible. There is nothing wrong with paying someone in cash and keeping it quiet, other than paying someone who should be an employee. But if you don't record the payment, you have no record and no proof of what transpired. If you are audited, the IRS can disallow any deduction that isn't recorded, even legal ones.

The term *off the books* means the same thing as under the table.

Expense category: If legal, depends on what the expense was for.

Unemployment Tax
Unemployment Insurance

Sole proprietors, partners in partnerships, and members (owners) of LLCs are not subject to federal unemployment tax. If you are required to pay state unemployment tax for yourself, it is deductible.

Unemployment insurance and unemployment tax are the same thing. The federal government. calls it a tax (FUTA, which stands for Federal Unemployment Tax Act), but many states call it insurance.

Employers pay federal unemployment tax (FUTA) for their employees. Some family employees are exempt from FUTA. See Family. Employers also may be required to pay a separate state unemployment tax/insurance for their employees. These taxes are deductible.

Expense category: Taxes and Licenses.

Uniforms

Uniforms used exclusively for work are deductible. This includes costumes and protective gear. Clothing with your company's logo or advertising is considered a uniform and is therefore deductible. Cost of cleaning is deductible.

Expense category: Supplies.

Unions

Dues and meetings are deductible.

Expense category: Other Expenses.

Political: If part of your union dues is for political lobbying, that portion of the dues is not deductible.

Unsalable Goods

Unsalable goods are deducted as part of inventory. See Inventory.

Expense category: Inventory.

Use Tax

Use tax is deductible.

Use tax is a type of sales tax. In states that have a sales tax, use tax is collected from businesses that made purchases without paying sales tax, such as an internet purchase or mail order purchase. Most large internet businesses collect sales tax, so there is no use tax on these transactions. Purchases for inventory are exempt from paying sales tax in most states, so there is also no use tax on these transactions. Use tax, when owed, is usually paid on state sales tax returns.

Normally, sales tax is added to the cost of the goods. But since the use tax is paid after the fact, most businesses deduct it as a business tax.

Expense category: Taxes and Licenses.

Highway Use Tax: There is a federal excise tax on truckers called a highway use tax. This is a completely different tax than the use tax described above. It also is deductible.

Expense category: Taxes and Licenses.

Utilities

Utilities, including electricity, gas, heating fuel, water, sewer service, garbage pickup, and any similar expenses, are deductible.

Expense category: Utilities.

Telephones come under different rules. See Cell Phones/Smartphones. Also see Telephone.

Renewable resources: You may be eligible for an Energy Tax Credit if you produce or use electricity from alternative sources. See Tax Credits.

Home-Based Business: Home utilities are part of the Home Expenses deduction, not deducted separately. See Home Expenses. Utilities do not include telephone, which can be deducted with limitations in addition to the home expenses. See Telephone.

Vacation

Can you write off part of your vacation as a business expense? Yes, if it is combined with a legitimate business trip and if you follow the rules. See Travel.

Vacation Facilities

The IRS has restrictions on vacation facilities, especially when made available to business owners and employees. If you own or lease a vacation facility, I suggest you talk to your accountant (who certainly will need to visit and examine the facility firsthand to be sure it meets all IRS requirements).

Expense category: Depends on what is being deducted.

IRS Red Flag Audit Warning: I doubt anything will catch an auditor's eye more quickly than a deduction for a vacation facility.

Businesses that operate vacation facilities do not come under these restrictions.

Vacation Pay

Vacation pay for employees is treated as regular taxable wages. See Wages.

Expense category: Wages.

Vandalism

Deductible to the extent not covered by insurance. See Casualty Losses.

Vans

You can deduct the cost of using a van for business, or you can take the Standard Mileage Rate, but with limitations. See Vehicles.

Vehicles

As confusing and complicated as some tax laws are, the IRS has outdone itself when it comes to tax deductions for vehicles. The vehicle laws are a monstrous mess of minutiae, as Spiro Agnew might have said. (Mr. Agnew was vice president of the United States under Richard Nixon, and was famous for calling people he didn't like "nattering nabobs of negativity." Vice President Agnew was forced to resign from office after pleading guilty to . . . tax fraud.)

Generally—and there are enough exceptions to fill a ten-yard dump truck—businesses can either deduct the actual expenses of purchasing and maintaining a vehicle, or can take a flat-rate Standard Mileage deduction for every mile driven for business.

These vehicle rules are for cars and trucks. These rules do not apply to tractors, construction machinery, or farm machinery. These types of heavy equipment are deducted as business asset. See Business Assets.

Deducting actual expenses: Actual expenses include the cost of the vehicle, which can be deducted the year of purchase or depreciated over five years. If you are renting or leasing a vehicle, you can deduct the payments (leases of 30 days or more have limitations). You can also deduct the costs to operate and maintain the vehicle, including fuel, oil changes, repairs, insurance, parking, tolls, garage rents, licenses, registration fees, even auto club dues.

Keeping itemized records of all your vehicle expenses is tedious work. The IRS realizes this also. In one of their rare helpful moods, they have come up with . . .

Standard Mileage Rate: Using this simple method, also known as the Standard Mileage Allowance, a business can deduct 65.5¢ per mile. This mileage rate is in lieu of all vehicle expenses except parking, tolls, interest (if you are paying an auto loan), and state and local taxes (other than sales tax on the vehicle), which are deductible in addition to the mileage rate. The rate changes, up or down a few cents, every year.

The Standard Mileage Rate can only be used, according to the IRS, for cars, vans, pickup trucks, and panel trucks. (No panel trucks have been manufactured in the last forty years.) You cannot use the Standard Mileage Rate for large trucks, RVs, busses, motorcycles, or construction equipment. You cannot use the Standard Mileage Rate if your business operates more than four vehicles at a time.

Part business, part personal: Vehicles used partly for business are prorated between business and nonbusiness use based on mileage. If you are using the Standard Mileage Rate, you can deduct the rate for every business mile driven. Keep in mind that commuting is considered nonbusiness and is not deductible. If you are deducting actual expenses, you can deduct a percentage of costs based on the percentage of business miles driven.

Mileage log: If you use a vehicle partly for business and partly for no business, the IRS requires you to keep a record of business versus nonbusiness miles driven. For the business miles, the record needs to include the date, time of day, destination, and business purpose. If you are audited and you don't have a logbook, or if you only have estimates or summaries, the IRS will disallow your deduction.

Vehicle ownership: If your business is a sole proprietorship, one-person LLC, spousal partnership, or joint venture, you can take a deduction for the business use of your personal vehicle. There is no need for the business to own the vehicle or register or insure the vehicle in the business name.

If your business is a partnership, corporation, or multi-owner LLC, to deduct expenses for a personal vehicle (one not owned by the business), the IRS requires that you have an Accountable Reimbursement Plan, a written policy that the vehicle use is business related and that the expenses are substantiated (you have receipts). Also, the partnership or LLC agreement or the corporate bylaws should include a clause requiring you to use your vehicle for business.

Which method?

You might want to figure your deduction under both methods to see which option gives you the highest tax deduction. If you have a new or expensive vehicle, keeping track of actual expenses will probably bring a bigger deduction than using the Standard Mileage Rate.

The deduction method you choose the first year you use your vehicle for business determines what method you can use in future years for that vehicle. If you deduct actual expenses the first year, you must stay with the actual-expenses method as long as you use that vehicle. If you use the Standard Mileage Rate the first year, you can switch back and forth if you want, using the Standard Mileage Rate some years and using the actual-expenses method other years (though not for leased vehicles).

Expense category: If you take the Standard Mileage Rate, Car and Truck Expenses. If you are deducting actual expenses, Car and Truck Expenses for all vehicle expenses except the cost of the vehicle itself. For buying a vehicle, Depreciation. If renting or leasing, Rent or Lease.

More information: IRS Publication 463, *Travel, Gift, and Car Expenses.*

Employers: Personal use of a company-owned vehicle by an employee is considered taxable wages to the employee, subject to all payroll taxes.

Tax Credits: Plug-in electric vehicles are eligible for a tax credit. See Tax Credits.

IRS Red Flag Audit Warning: See the mileage log requirement above. This is one of the few things the IRS almost always checks when auditing small businesses. Also, IRS agents know that it's rare for an individual to actually use a vehicle 100% for business, so people who claim 100% business use of a vehicle increase their audit chances.

If you drive a car, I'll tax the street. If you take a walk, I'll tax your feet.

—Taxman G. Harrison

Vending Carts
Vending Machines

Vending machines and vending carts can be deducted the year purchased and first used in the business, or at your option, depreciated over seven years. For details and special situations, see Business Assets.

Expense category: Depreciation or Other Expenses, depending on several factors. See Business Assets.

Vineyards

See Farming.

Virtual Currency

See Cryptocurrency.

Voided Checks

I hope it's obvious that you do not get a deduction for a voided check you wrote and then tore up. If you don't void the check immediately, and you've already taken a deduction for it, reverse the deduction out of your records. Also see Bounced Checks.

Wages

If your business is not a corporation, your own wages—that is, the wages you pay yourself if you pay yourself a wage—are not a deductible business expense. See Draw and Paying Yourself. If your business is a partnership, also see Guaranteed Payments to Partners. If your business is a corporation, you are an employee of your business like any other employee, and your salary is deductible.

Employers: Employee wages are deductible. See Fringe Benefits. Also see Payroll Taxes.

Expense category: Wages.

More information: IRS Publication 15, *Employer's Tax Guide*.

Tax credits: There are several tax credits available to employers. See Tax Credits.

The Internal Revenue Service

Warehouse

The cost of renting a warehouse is deductible. The cost of a building you own can be depreciated. Some storage buildings can be deducted the year of purchase. See Buildings.

Expense category: If rented or leased, Rent or Lease. If owned, Depreciation.

More information: For buildings you own, IRS Publication 946, *How to Depreciate Property*.

Home-Based Business: A warehouse in the home is part of the Home Expenses deduction, not deducted separately. See Home Expenses.

Warranties

Extended warranties that cost additional money are deductible if they do not extend beyond twelve months. If they exceed twelve months, see Prepayments.

Expense category: Repairs and Maintenance.

Watchdog

Deductible. See Guard Dog.

Water

Water and other utilities are deductible.

Expense category: Utilities.

Also see Drilling.

Home-Based Business: Utilities are part of the Home Expenses deduction, not deducted separately. See Home Expenses.

Watercraft

See Boats.

Website

The cost of designing and setting up a website is deductible. If the initial design cost is significant (over $2,500), it may have to be amortized over three years. See Depreciation. Domain name registration, hosting fees, and costs of maintaining a website are deductible. The cost of internet access is fully deductible if used only for business. If used partly for business, you prorate the cost and deduct only the business portion.

Expense category: Office Expenses. If amortizing, Other Expenses.

Wells

See Drilling.

Wife on Payroll

See Spouse.

Work Clothes

Deductible only if unsuitable for street wear or if it is a uniform. See Uniforms. Clothing with your company's logo or advertising is fully deductible, even though the clothing may be suitable for street wear. Cost of cleaning work clothes is deductible.

Expense category: Supplies.

Workers' Compensation Insurance

Workers' compensation insurance (workers' comp) for yourself is deductible only if your state requires you to have workers' compensation insurance on yourself. If the coverage is voluntary, the premiums are not deductible.

Employers: Workers' compensation insurance an employer pays to cover employees is deductible.

Expense category: Insurance.

Work in Process

Work in process, also called work in progress, is a manufacturing term for a product that is partially completed. Work in process is part of your inventory. See Inventory.

Expense category: Inventory.

Work Opportunity Tax Credit

Tax credit for hiring certain disadvantaged employees. Expires after 2025. See Tax Credits.

Expense category: Tax credits are taken on Form 1040, not on the business part of the tax return.

Workshop

The cost of renting a workshop is deductible. The cost of a building you own can be depreciated. See Buildings.

Expense category: If rented or leased, Rent or Lease. If owned, Depreciation.

More information: For buildings you own, IRS Publication 946, *How to Depreciate Property*.

Home-Based Business: A workshop in the home is part of the Home Expenses deduction, not deducted separately. See Home Expenses.

Worthless Goods

Worthless inventory can be written off if it wasn't deducted when purchased.

Expense category: Inventory.

Worthless business assets that were deducted when purchased cannot be deducted a second time. If the assets are being depreciated, the remaining undepreciated balance can be deducted.

Expense category: Depreciation.

It is our Patriotic Duty to keep as much money out of the hands of our government as we can.

—Philosopher Walter Camp

Yellow Pages

Yes, Virginia, there is still a Yellow Pages. Yellow Pages listings and advertising are deductible.

Expense category: Advertising.

Zoning

Costs of zoning permits, filings, hearings, appeals, and petitions are deductible, with two important exceptions.

Zoning costs associated with building construction are added to the cost of the building and depreciated. Zoning costs associated with land rezoning, such as residential to industrial, are added to the cost of the land and cannot be deducted until the land is sold.

Expense category: If not part of building construction or land rezoning, Taxes and Licenses.

Home-Based Business: Any zoning costs are part of the Home Expenses deduction, not deducted separately. See Home Expenses.

Small business is where we have the most trouble.

—Former IRS Commissioner Charles O. Rossotti

Drive ahead, don't spare the steam, make all the noise possible, and by all means, keep down the expenses.

—P. T. Barnum